WILLIAM LAMBARDE, ELIZABETHAN JURIST

1536–1601

WILBUR DUNKEL

WILLIAM LAMBARDE, ELIZABETHAN JURIST 1536–1601

RUTGERS UNIVERSITY PRESS

New Brunswick   *New Jersey*

"Historians Courageous," by Catherine Drinker Bowen, originally appeared in *Proceedings* of the American Philosophical Society, Vol. 101, No. 3 (June 1957). It is reprinted here with the permission of the author and of *Proceedings* of the American Philosophical Society.

For

GEORGIA OSBORN DUNKEL

ACKNOWLEDGMENTS

To Catherine Drinker Bowen for the use of "Historians Courageous," I am particularly indebted; her view of Lambarde among the antiquarians illumines an important aspect of Elizabethan activity.

To the Administration of the University of Rochester, and to my colleagues, I am grateful for the scholarly leaves that made possible my study; in particular to Provost McCrea Hazlett and the Committee on Grants-in-Aid; and I am very indebted to Librarian John R. Russell and members of the staff for borrowing and purchasing rare books.

As the repository of nearly all the important Lambarde manuscripts and first editions, the Folger Shakespeare Library in Washington, D.C., provided stimulation as well as material. As everyone who has ever worked there knows, it has truly become a community of scholars. Under the direction of Dr. Louis B. Wright and his staff of experts, the Folger Shakespeare Library affords an exchange of ideas and learning. And so to the visiting scholars who contributed to my work, my deepest thanks. I am mindful that Dr. Wright arranged a grant for me for a sustained period of study; Dr. Giles Dawson guided me to manuscripts and records;

both Dr. James G. McManaway and Miss Dorothy Mason, among others, gave assistance to me on innumerable occasions.

I must record my appreciation of aid given to me in locating manuscripts and fugitive items in England. Dr. Felix Hull, Archivist for the County of Kent, was particularly helpful, as were my colleagues at Hull University during my year as a visiting professor.

My thanks go to my daughter, Mrs. Patricia Johnston, for typing my manuscript, to my wife for patience in listening and reading, and to Miss Elizabeth Otis for counsel.

CONTENTS

HISTORIANS COURAGEOUS

CATHERINE DRINKER BOWEN

In the year 1572, a certain society was formed in London. Its members were scholars, interested primarily in the history of England. Inviting the Archbishop of Canterbury to be their patron, they named their new sodality *The Society of Antiquaries*, and began at once to hold weekly supper meetings, with papers read and discussion later in the evening.

The Society was to be memorable not only for its scholarly activities *per se*, but because of the strong effect these activities had upon the political thinking of the day. The year 1572 was, of course, the fourteenth year of Queen Elizabeth's reign, when England, as yet, scarcely dared call herself a nation—sixteen years before the Spanish Armada was sighted off the coast of Devon, and routed and beaten and sunk by the Royal Navy and a beautifully persistent series of hurricanes. A generation later—indeed, a century later—men still spoke of the year '88 with pride, in something of the tone our own founding fathers, in their old age, used to speak of 1776, as the sacred year in which a nation had its birth.

When a nation is born and learns to speak, one of its first expressed desires seems to be the desire for a past, for a national history, recorded and set down that he who runs may read, proof positive that the nation is a nation, with a deep foundation on which its future can build. So it was with the England of Elizabeth. One year after the Armada victory, the Society of Antiquaries applied to the Queen for a charter of incorporation and for some public building where they might assemble and have a library, "well furnished with scarce books, original charters, muniments and other mss." [1] Members offered to take the Oath of Supremacy to Elizabeth, to show that they contemplated nothing subversive, and a second oath to preserve the library.

As always with the inspiration and beginning of great movements, the originators of the Society were men of parts. The dean of them all was John Stow, compiler of the volumes entitled *Annals of England. Faithfully collected out of the most authenticall Authors, Records and other Monuments of Antiquity from the first inhabitation until 1592.* Stow, who lived and died in poverty, was a cheerful scholar who trudged on foot to find his records—perhaps the most accurate of English chroniclers and sixteenth-century annalists. Stow's *Survey of London* is a book of immense value to the historian or biographer of Elizabethan times. Street by street it tells where everybody lived, describes the wards and liberties, the towers and castles of the old city, with bits and oddments of gossip included on the way. From his house, says Stow, he can hear every Thursday, the gunners from the Tower of London practice with their brass pieces in the Artillery Yard at Hogge Lane nearby. He is disgusted because archers and bowmen nowadays (*circa* 1590) instead of standing in Finsbury Field to shoot with the manly English longbow, "creep into bowling allies and ordinary dicing houses nearer home, where they hazard . . . their money at unlawful games." [2]

Such items possess more than mere charm and quaintness. They are the very stuff of which social history is made. It was the Society of Antiquaries that fostered the plan of walking

[1] Introduction: containing an historical account of the origin and establishment of the Society of Antiquaries, *Archaeologia* i :i–xliii, 1779.

[2] Stow, John, *A survey of London* 1 :104, Oxford, Clarendon Press, 1908.

through the shires and counties of England, to record and
preserve antiquities discovered therein: Roman coins, Anglo
Saxon artifacts, whatever contributed to the history of England. Heretofore, local chronicles had not been dignified by
the names of history. To educated gentlemen of the sixteenth
century, history meant classical history—Herodotus, Xeno-
phon, Thucydides, books written in a "more respectable"
language than the native tongue.

William Lambarde, thirty-six years old when the Society
of Antiquaries was formed, for some reason is always spoken
of as "old Lambarde." Lambarde had read law at Lincoln's
Inn; he translated the Anglo-Saxon laws into Latin. Before
he was thirty, Lambarde had walked through his native
county and written his observations, entitled *A Perambulation
of Kent*. Named Justice of the Peace, Lambarde, out of his
experiences and no doubt from desire for authoritative direction concerning the office, compiled his *Eirenarcha*, or, *Of the
Office of Justice of the Peace*. Later he wrote *Archion*, or *a
Commentary upon the High Courts of Justice in England*.
Both books for long remained the standard authority. Queen
Elizabeth liked Lambarde and named him Keeper of the
Records in the Rolls Chapel and the Tower of London.
When Queen and scholar both were approaching seventy,
Lambarde presented Elizabeth with a book descriptive of the
documents under his charge. It is characteristic of that great
Queen that as she paged over the book she read passages
aloud, stopped to ask the meaning of technical phrases and
remarked that she "would be a scholar in her age and thought
it no scorn to learn during her life, being of the mind of that
philosopher, who in his last years began with the Greek
alphabet." [3]

Lambarde, like others of the Antiquarian Society, was a

[3] Neale, John E., *Queen Elizabeth*, 381, London, Jonathan Cape, 1934.

pioneer in his work on the laws—a pioneer in that he was not content to take his history from the schoolmen and medieval authorities, but went to the records. In his *Archion* there is a revealing, proud little sentence. It comes after lengthy quotations from Matthew Paris and that much cited and rather doubtful historian, Polydore Vergil. Lambarde breaks off and remarks suddenly, "But what need I to hang long upon the credit of historians, seeing that from this time downward the authentick records of the Parliaments do offer me present helpe?" [4]

The authentic records—It is a phrase that we hear again and again from these scholars who were, as I have said, in a sense the pioneers of our modern so-called scientific history. There is no need to describe here the meaning of the English Renaissance, the fresh approach to art and literature, the new pride in a national language, the discarding of old forms and the sloughing off of medieval dust. Yet in all our celebration of the Renaissance Man, the Elizabethan Man, I think the historians are too often forgotten. Old Lambarde is forgotten, who was so young when he sat poring over Anglo-Saxon documents, not content to take history second hand. Even William Camden is neglected, who wrote the fascinating book called *Annales, or the History of the Most Renowned and Victorious Princesse Elizabeth, Late Queen of England.* Camden, a vivid writer, was eye witness to many of the events he describes. He saw the Earl of Essex tried for treason in Westminster Hall and portrayed the scene in all its tragic pageantry. "These things," he writes, "whereat I was present myself, I have with uncorrupted fidelity compendiously related." [5] Like Lambarde, William Camden traveled over the countryside, setting down what he could find of history and

[4] Lambarde, William, *Archion*, 266, London, printed for Daniel Frère, 1635.

[5] Camden, William, *Annales*, 549, London, printed for Benjamin Fisher.

the beginnings of things. *Britannia,* his book was called; it went through many editions. Camden was a gentle, happy man, strong and active physically, a scholar with a good digestion, independent minded, who refused knighthood, declaring that in all his life he "never made suit to any man." [6]

It is an extraordinary roster of names, this list of antiquaries: William Hakewill, barrister, who wrote *Modus Tenendi Parliamentum,* or *The Old Manner of Holding Parliaments in England*—and thereby helped to stabilize procedure in both Houses. Whether in Parliament or in the courtroom, small matters of procedure—how and when the vote is taken, how committees are named—can mean, for ordinary citizens, the difference between bondage and freedom. Hakewill's book is an essentially practical volume, small enough to put in one's pocket; it has a forthright style that is appealing. In describing how the Lord Chancellor, on opening day, pronounces the causes for which Parliament has been called: "The Lord Chancellor shall stand," says Hakewill, "so that all of the Parliament might hear him that speaketh, or, if he speak something darkly, or talk in a low voice, let him speak again, and speak louder also, or let another speak for him." [7] Hakewill was a cousin to Sir Thomas Bodley, collector of the famous library at Oxford.

Among these antiquaries, we owe to one studious and stiffnecked Puritan lawyer most of our knowledge of the last four Parliaments of Elizabeth. Sir Simonds D'Ewes was a born scholar who liked to read history in his coach while traveling; when alone he read in Latin; if he had a companion he read aloud in English. D'Ewes sat in many Parliaments and col-

[6] Thompson, Edward Maunde, William Camden, *Dict. Natl. Biog.* 3:729–737.

[7] Hakewill, William, *Modus tenendi parliamentum,* 13, London, printed for Abel Roper, 1671.

lected and printed such diaries and records as he could find, supplementing these, in his autobiography, with enthusiastically malicious pen portraits of everybody who was anybody. Concerning legal history of England, D'Ewes tells us that at first he studied the records only to find matter of law that might help to win his cases. "But afterwards perceiving other excellences might be observed from them, both historical and national," [8] he pursued learning for its own sake. Considering D'Ewes' character—quarrelsome, over-pious—it is touching that on the day that his little twin sons died he should have written, "To mitigate and moderate this sorrow, I fell close to my sweet and satisfying studies." [9]

It would be pleasant to describe the full list of members of the old Antiquarian Society, brave and patient scholars who traveled by land or water down to the Tower of London, and in the damp and nauseous cold, copied and wrote and studied the authentic records of English history. It would be good to pause over John Selden the great legal scholar, dark haired, dashing, irresistible to the ladies, he who said we should avoid "the sterile part of antiquity." In Parliament, when bills proposed by the Commons were quashed by the Lords, Selden fought back nobly. "The House of Commons," he remarked characteristically, "is called yᵉ Lower House in Twenty Acts of Parliamt. But what are twenty Acts of Parliamt, amongst frends?" [10] Passionately opposed to clerical pretensions, Selden was a thorn in the side of the Assembly of Divines. "He was wont to mock them," wrote a contemporary, "about their little gilt Bibles, and would baffle and vexe them sadly: Sayd he, 'I doe consider

[8] D'Ewes, Sir Simonds, *The autobiography and correspondence* 1:235, London, Richard Bentley, 1845.

[9] *Ibid.* 2:90.

[10] Haskins, George L., *The growth of English representative government*, 126, Philadelphia, University of Pennsylvania Press, 1948.

the original,' for he was able to runne them all downe with
his Greeke and Antiquities." [11] One of Selden's anti-clerical
books was recalled from the press by James I, who summoned
the author to the palace and forced him to sign an apology.
"I profess still to all the world," Selden said later, "that I
am sorry for it. . . . But is there a syllable in my book of
less truth because I am sorry for the publishing of it?" [12]
Selden's library is now part of the Bodleian; we are told that,
when the librarians were sorting and arranging, on opening
Selden's books they found several pairs of spectacles, which
their owner apparently had put in to keep his place, and forgotten. In every volume that he acquired, Selden caused the
words to be written in Greek, "In all things, above all things,
liberty." [13]

Amid these prickly, spiny historians, hot for their rights
as citizens, it is pleasing to come upon Sir Henry Spelman,
a good-natured country gentleman of estate, High Sheriff of
Norfolk, who moved to London so that he might be near
the world of books. Sir Henry's chief historical interest was
the Church of England, but he wrote also a description of
Norfolk, *Icenia sive Norfoleiae Descriptio topographica,* and
published a glossary of Latin and Anglo-Saxon law words.
Incidentally, Spelman was a member of the Council for New
England, drew up their patents in 1620, and performed other
legal work rising out of their struggles with the Virginia
Company. A friendly scholar, Sir Henry helped and encouraged others in their work and was very active in all affairs of
the Society of Antiquaries—the kind of man without whom

[11] Aubrey, John, *Aubrey's brief lives,* ed. Oliver Lawson Dick, 272,
Secker and Warburg, 1950.

[12] Johnson, George W., *Memoirs of John Selden,* 69, London, Orr and
Smith, 1835.

[13] Gooch, George Peabody, and Harold J. Laski, *English democratic ideas
in the seventeenth century,* 104, Cambridge, Univ. Press, 1927.

learned societies could not exist, a genial gentleman, willing to keep the minutes, plan dinners and symposia, search out new members and generally feed the fires when interest falls off.

The Society of Antiquaries had as it were two lives, one during its official existence under Queen Elizabeth, and another very unofficial life after 1603, under James I and his son. The history of England, as the antiquaries unearthed it, did not favor the divine right of kings, a theory which James brought with him from Scotland and in which he fervently believed. James had trouble with nearly every Parliament that met in his reign, and so, of course did his son, Charles. The sovereign, James liked to say, was above the law, free of the law, *legibus solutus*. Chief Justice Coke, foremost of antiquarian lawyers, retorted by quoting Bracton, the great thirteenth-century judge: "The King is under God and the laws." [14] James told Parliament angrily that there were kings before there were laws or Parliament either, to which the antiquaries had not one answer but half a dozen, all stemming from ancient English authors whose names the monarch had probably never heard until he crossed the border down from Scotland. When James wished, for instance, to profit from certain traditional revenues technically called *impositions*, the House of Commons, by this time teeming with lawyers, fished up precedents and citations concerning the illegality of impositions. They did the same with the royal monopolies, a form of political plum which the Tudors, like James, had found most useful in rewarding their courtiers and followers.

The Society of Antiquaries had a superbly convenient meeting place during these early Stuart years. One of their

[14] Coke, Sir Edward, 12 *Report*, 65 f., The Savoy, E. and R. Nutt and R. Gosling, 1738.

most celebrated members, Sir Robert Cotton, had established himself in a pleasant dwelling next door to Parliament, with a walled garden leading to the Thames. Cotton's library of books, manuscripts, seals and coins was known far beyond England. European scholars corresponded with him; the English nuns of Cambray begged books for their convent library. Casaubon, the great French classicist, came often to visit Cotton. Sir Francis Bacon borrowed manuscripts. Sir Walter Raleigh, imprisoned in the Tower of London, sent for a certain old parchment, perhaps in preparation for his *History of the World*.

Everyone borrowed from Cotton's library. When William Camden the annalist died, his will declared that "Sir Robert Cotton shall have the first view of my books, that he may take out such as I borrowed of him." [15] From one scholar to another, could there be a pleasanter posthumous greeting? Not everyone made such honorable restitution, but this, happily, was somewhat equalized by the fact that Cotton himself borrowed books anywhere and everywhere. It was rumored that when authorities in the muniment rooms refused Cotton a document, he slipped the parchment beneath his doublet and carried it home. Fortunately for scholarship, Cotton was a rich man, and so passionate about the history of his country that when he spoke of it his words came too fast, and he stuttered. His portrait shows a large, beaked nose, the scholar's frown, and a somehow unquenchable look of vitality. Sir Simonds D'Ewes, the Puritan, records that Cotton, when old, "having been for divers years together a miserable pursuer of his lust . . . drank sack in which snakes were dissolved, being commonly called viper wine, to restore nature." [16] Considering that the writer admitted to many borrowings of

[15] Thompson, *op. cit.*
[16] D'Ewes, *op. cit.* 2:39.

Cottoniana, this seems more than a little unkind, even for a Puritan.

But vitality is a valuable trait in a scholar and historian. Behold, then, the Society of Antiquaries, many of them members of Parliament, hurrying downstairs from their respective legislative chambers to walk through a narrow door into Cotton's library, there to gather precedents to suit the purpose. Never was a monarch so plagued by history and historians as was James I. William Lambarde was dead. But his *Archion* was cited, to prove that in England, power had never lain with the King alone, but in the three estates, king, nobility, and commons. This, said Lambarde, was true even before the Conquest. When the proper charters were not on Cotton's shelves, younger scholars were sent to the Tower to fetch them. A whole bouquet of glorious Lancastrian freedoms was gathered, a thorny, spicy nosegay for presentation to Stuart kings. And if historians today look upon these Lancastrian freedoms as something of a myth, still, they served their purpose nobly. The particular effectiveness of legality by precedent, liberty by precedent, lies in the fact that it is not revolutionary. The liberties of England, said our antiquarian lawyers, need not be devised anew. Bills lately proposed in Parliament were, the lawyers declared, in no sense innovations—a word hateful alike to king and lawyer. Merely, these bills expressed the ancient liberties of England, which needed to be "restored." In the year 1765, John Adams and James Otis had a like watchword, when Otis argued in Massachusetts against the Writs of Assistance, and quoted Sir Edward Coke on Magna Carta. Lawyers are naturally conservative. If change must be accomplished, they choose history as their guide, in preference to destruction and a total sweeping-out, believing perhaps that fact and experience carry more conviction than the fluty voice of a newly erected Goddess of Reason. "The lawyers," wrote Maitland, imbued with "a new spirit, fought the battle of the constitution against James and Charles, and historical research appeared as the guardian of national liberties. That the Stuarts united against themselves three such men as Edward Coke, John Selden and William Prynne, is the measure of their folly and their failure." [17]

The historians whom I describe were not only learned. They were clever, far from unworldly, and remarkably eloquent. In 1614 King James, almost beside himself, declared that "if he would hunt what other kinges have don, he might find somwhat for himself, although there be antiquaries and nymble wittes in the house." [18] That same year, the Society had only one official meeting. Before they could hold a second, King James dissolved them. William Hakewill, known to his compatriots as a "master of precedents," was arrested.

In any time and clime, it is dangerous to try to silence scholars. When these scholars are lawyers, the hazard increases. From now on our antiquaries, though disbanded and unfrocked, were busier than ever. During the famous Parliaments of the 1620's, Sir Robert Cotton's library saw an influx of new adherents. Young men, fierce for liberty: Sir John Eliot of Yorkshire came there, and William Prynne the Puritan, who lost his ears for pamphleteering, a scholar whose output was amazing, about two hundred books and pamphlets, calculated by a contemporary as a sheet produced for every day of Prynne's life since manhood. "His manner of Studie," wrote a friend, "was thus: He wore a long quilt cap which came 2 or 3, at least, inches over his eies, which served him as an umbrella to defend his Eies from the light. About every three houres his man was to bring him a roll and a

---

[17] Maitland, Frederic W., *Encyclopedia Britannica*, 11th ed., 9:600–607, "English Law."

[18] Notestein, Wallace, Frances Relf and Hartley Simpson, *Commons debates 1621* 7:app. C, 647, New Haven, Yale Univ. Press, 1935.

pot of Ale to refocillate his wasted spirits: so he studied and dranke and munched some bread; and this maintained him till night, and then, he made a good Supper." [19]

In 1625 King James died, to be succeeded by that very attractive young prince, his son, Charles I. In Charles's Parliaments of 1626 and 1627, the scholars continued their work, making the bridge between law and history, which, ever since, has been strong and significant in the United States as in England. On occasion, in support of their principles, the antiquaries may have stretched their historical points a trifle; Edward Coke's detractors have said that he "invented" Magna Carta. At a time when that great charter of liberties was forgotten or neglected, Coke dug it out and read it aloud to his law students in the early mornings—in Latin—and to the House of Commons also, especially that noble Chapter 39, which opens, "*Nullus liber homo.* . . . No freeman shall be taken, or imprisoned, or disseised . . . of his liberties . . . but by the lawful judgment of his peers or by the law of the land."

"Magna Charta," Coke told the Parliament of 1628, "Magna Charta is such a fellow that he will have no sovereign." [20]

It was this same Parliament which presented to King Charles the great Petition of Right that served as model for our Revolutionary forefathers at the Continental Congress. And it was the antiquaries, meeting unofficially in Cotton's library, who formed the strong policy needed to carry the great Petition through the House. There were five men at that famous pre-Parliament meeting, among them Edward Coke, John Eliot, and John Selden. Of the five, all but one were imprisoned for their pains. "Mr. John Selden, my great

[19] Aubrey, *op. cit.*, 251.

[20] Rushworth, John, *Historical collections* 1:562, London, D. Browne (etc.), 1721.

friend while he lived," wrote a contemporary, "was clapt up because, being a member of the House of Commons, he had preferred the danger of telling truth, before the safety of silence." [21] Sir Edward Coke was seventy when they took him down the river to the Tower; he stayed there for six cold, miserable months. Sir John Eliot was never released, but died in the Tower after six years' imprisonment, aged forty.

There remains to tell of Sir Robert Cotton's fate—he of the viper wine and the glorious library by the Thames that served as a school to so many. In the second year of Charles's reign, a news writer stated that "Sir Robert Cotton's books are threatened to be taken away, because he is accused of imparting ancient precedents to the lower house." [22] Three years later, Cotton's library was sealed up by royal command, and commissioners were sent to search it and note everything which concerned affairs of state. Cotton petitioned for pardon and restitution of his books. When he had no reply, his health failed; he told his friends that "they had broken his heart, that had locked up his library from him." [23] He petitioned a second time, saying that his documents were "perishing for lack of airing, and that no one was allowed to consult them." [24] Sir Simonds D'Ewes, the Puritan, called on Cotton, and reported that sorrow had changed Sir Robert's countenance, "formerly ruddy and well-coloured . . . into a grim blackish paleness, near to the resemblance and hue of a dead visage." [25] Cotton himself told the King's officers that "their

[21] Johnson, *op. cit.*, 99.

[22] Birch, Thomas, *The court and times of Charles the First* 1:98, London, Henry Colburn, 1848.

[23] D'Ewes, *op. cit.* 2:41.

[24] Lee, Sir Sidney, Sir Robert Bruce Cotton, *Dict. Natl. Biog.* 4:1233–1240.

[25] D'Ewes, *op. cit.* 2:42.

so long detaining his books from him, without rendering any
reason for the same, had been the cause of his mortal mal-
ady." [26] A few weeks later, he was dead.

It has been said that no man dies for love. Yet here is one
historian who quite literally died of love for his books when
they were taken from him. All honor then, to these brave
scholars who endured hardship and prison for their works,
scholars who surely merit the phrase *Historians Courageous*.

[26] Mr. Pory to Sir Thomas Puckering, Bart., 12 May 1631, in Birch,
op. cit. 2:112.

WILLIAM LAMBARDE, ELIZABETHAN JURIST
1536–1601

Doe equall right to rich and poor,
    as wit and law extends;
Give none advice in any cause,
    that you before depends:
Your Sessions hold as statutes bid:
    the forfeits that befall;
See entered well, and then estreat
    them to the Chequer all:
Receive no fee, but that is given
    by King, good use, or right:
No precept send to party self,
    but to indifferent wight.

William Lambarde,
Eirenarcha, Bk. I

Chapter 1

THE MAN (1536–1601)

William Lambarde, author of books on courts of law and the first county history of Kent, was a stalwart supporter of Queen Elizabeth I of England. Three years younger than Her Majesty, he was beginning his first book when the young Queen ascended the throne in 1558. His career as a justice in Kent, deputy for lords of her Privy Council, and as a Master in the high court in Chancery paralleled her long and complex reign. But if ever a man walked through the confusion of religious and political turmoil that characterized Queen Elizabeth's England without ever thinking of preferment and rewards, such a man was William Lambarde. He dared to disagree with the Queen while he served as a Member of Parliament. He had the audacity to correct in print the errors of the Lord Chancellor. And, at a time when crime was rampant, he struggled against the opinion of his betters to obtain equal justice for the poor and rich alike in the administration of criminal justice.

Lambarde was an individualist and an innovator. While he was still a student at Lincoln's Inn he compiled the first collection of the customs and laws of ancient Kent and translated them from the Anglo-Saxon language into Latin. At the same time, having inherited a manor in Kent from his father, a rich London merchant, he began the systematic survey of that county, and from his notes he wrote the first history of any county in England. He built and endowed the first Protestant hospital for the poor—he called it a "college"—which attracted so much interest that persons unknown to him left legacies for its endowment. Others, in particular Lord Cobham, emulated him by leaving large sums of money for the erection, furnishing, and endowment of similar institutions for the worthy poor.

Lambarde began what might have been the first topographical history of England and Wales but gave it up when William Camden's *Britannia* appeared to be nearing completion before his own work had progressed as far. While his history of the office of justice of the peace and manual for conducting the duties of this office was not the first, it was the most useful and complete book of its kind, superseding the old and thus requiring reprinting, reediting, and enlargement seven times during his lifetime and six times after his death. He wrote the first manual for the use of parish officers, such as constables, to assist them in performing their precise duties. These two manuals were not only useful and necessary, but were also means to standarizing procedures in local government. Since Queen Elizabeth I, like her forbears, placed great emphasis upon local government and increased the powers of the justices of the peace, Lambarde's contribution at this particular time can scarcely be overestimated. For more than a quarter century his manual defined the procedures, clarifying statutes, ordinances, and confused statements of the responsibilities of justices in the commissions of the peace. Lambarde accomplished this monumental task while actively participating for some twenty years as a justice of the peace.

Perhaps *Archeion,* his history of the high courts of England, represents his finest research and study. The increased powers of the justices of the peace seemed in certain cases to overlap the work of the itinerate justices from the King's Bench, who conducted the Assizes twice a year on their scheduled rounds. The increased power of the prerogative Court of Star Chamber, the Court of Requests, and the ancient expression of the sovereign's mercy through the Lord Chancellor in the high Court in Chancery led in Lambarde's time to an intense quarrel between the courts of common law in Westminster and these prerogative high courts. This was the great issue in legal justice that Lambarde surveyed, but his book was not printed until thirty-four years after his death. He had unfortunately offered to dedicate it to the unworthy Robert Cecil, the son of the great Lord Burghley. Scribes and secretaries evidently made copies of this manuscript, as in Sir Roger Twysden's collection; nevertheless its influence developed in the seventeenth century.

Lambarde's work with manuscripts and records from ancient times made his writings authoritative. It was, furthermore, the kind of scholarly and contemplative work appropriate for a man with a considerable fortune and no need to justify himself in the eyes of his neighbors or the distinguished peers at the court. He enjoyed the countryside and Irish-bred horses, his only extravagance. He purchased books on agriculture and put his information to productive use; he acquired books on breeding sheep and cattle. He knew a great deal about beekeeping and appraisal of land and evidently was a shrewd dealer in buying and leasing manors and farms. And not least was his ability to speak to the farmers in Kent, not only as a learned man whom they could respect but with understanding of their problems. All this knowledge became useful in the reports that he wrote while Lord Burghley's deputy in the Alienations Office.

Lambarde's studying and writing indicate the wide scope

of his interests and can be explained as within the training and experience of a learned common lawyer. It is more difficult to account for his adding to these duties by becoming a crusading justice of the peace, with particular concern for the poor. Yet assumption of the additional duties characterizes the man. During this period there were no longer religious establishments for the care of the sick and needy, since Parliament had enacted statutes for the gradual dissolution of the monastic holdings. Nothing practicable had as yet been formulated for the care of the poor, except the parish poor boxes and levies to assist the parish officers in providing minimum relief. Vagabonds roamed the highways and became thieves and robbers. They were branded and whipped and sent on to the next county without solution of their problems. The vicious and lazy ones came before the justices of the peace and were sentenced to jail. But the sick were dependent upon such bounty as they could beg, as the gentry had become accustomed to having the poor always with them.

Lambarde was no sentimentalist about the poor. He was stern in his punishment of those who apparently did not want to work, but he led his fellow justices in Kent to erect and maintain a House of Correction, in which the poor rogues and wenches who had been convicted of misdemeanors and felonies could learn some trade or useful occupation. Such rehabilitation of criminals came in Kent, largely through Lambarde's thinking on the problem, years before Parliament accepted this responsibility and began to enact a series of poor laws to deal with the problem.

Lambarde was practical in his thinking about criminal law, recognizing that rich persons could retain lawyers and sustain the cost of protracted litigation but that poor persons were without defense. He knew that neighbors usually found it to their advantage not to report misdemeanors or felonies committed by powerful acquaintances. Everyone then was familiar with bribes for both witnesses and judges. The jurors who reported at the quarter sessions seldom mentioned their neighbors unless to be vindictive. Envy and covetousness, slander and false witness, were so common that the system of local government could be and was ridiculed.

To contravene the low opinion of local justice, Lambarde not only assisted the justices of the peace with his manual but also instructed the jurors at the quarter sessions by carefully writing and delivering lengthy sermons on the significance of their oaths and duties. Twenty-nine of these Charges to the Jurors are extant in fine legal script with interlinear insertions and signed by him in Anglo-Saxon script; one other exists in printed form. These were not perfunctory addresses. On the contrary, Lambarde expressed his philosophy of the English law and his religious convictions in an endeavor to inspire the jurors to report misdemeanors and felonies committed in the areas of the county from which they had come to the quarter sessions or special commissions.

On occasion he addressed them as a father speaking to wayward children and in later years as the elder statesman, the Master in Chancery, returning home to talk to his neighbors and friends about local conditions that must be improved. But there was always a righteous indignation because they had failed to report evildoers in their respective communities, for these grand jurors—he called them "inquiring jurors"— provided the information for these hearings and determinations. Sometimes he had reports from Secretary Walsingham and the Lord Baron of the Exchequer; then he would examine the jurors to find out if they had withheld this information.

Lambarde was a devoutly religious man, of the flesh and blood of which martyrs are made. Living ever in the eyes of his God, he was paradoxically both humble and certain of his convictions. In God's universe, the natural law was order.

He therefore could accept without apparent questioning that the sovereign of England was God's anointed deputy; that the English laws were good; and that the spiritual and political isolation of England from Europe would lead to peace, even though he did advocate trade with Europe. He did not question that the "good" might be different from the status quo, except in his desire to improve the administration of the good laws of England in accord with God's orderly universe. So the nature of the "good" was plain as a pikestaff: the good people observed the laws and maintained order, the evil persons committed misdemeanors and felonies and thus disturbed the peace.

In his domestic life Lambarde did not question God's benevolence to man. Even the death of his very young first wife did not destroy his faith, although he apparently loved her dearly. Some years later when he married again he apparently was devoted to his second wife who was able to give him the heir that he wanted. When she died, leaving him with four small children, he was grief-stricken but unshaken in his faith. Here again appeared the paradox, as in the Christian religion, for it was his love of God and his conscience that encouraged him to alleviate the pitiable condition of the poor, among whom he differentiated between the indolent and the afflicted.

Both Lambarde and Queen Elizabeth had grown up amidst religious turbulence. In the year of Lambarde's birth, Elizabeth's mother, Anne Boleyn, was convicted of adultery and beheaded in the Tower of London. Elizabeth's father, King Henry VIII, had separated the English church from Rome in 1534, with the Act of Supremacy, thus disturbing the hierarchy of the clergy as well as certain basic concepts of faith. Later Parliament passed statutes bringing about the dissolution of monastic establishments. As a result of these statutes vast estates of the church became acreages of land to be sold

to individual farmers, gifts to the King's friends and syco-
phants, and choice additions of real estate in the possession
of the Crown. This division of the spoils provided in later
years additional work for common lawyers.

When King Henry VIII died, his ten-year-old son,
Edward VI, succeeded to the throne, and during the six-year
Protestant Protectorate, from 1547 to 1553, religious observ-
ances were further complicated. King Edward VI was succeeded by his half sister, Queen Mary, who married King
Philip II of Spain, and during her reign the Roman Catholic
allegiances were resumed from 1553 to 1558. On Queen
Mary's death Elizabeth succeeded her half sister, and an-
nounced that she would resume the separation of the English
church from Rome, following the procedures of her father,
King Henry VIII. So once again the faithful had to revise
their practices.

William Lambarde was twenty-two when Queen Elizabeth I ascended the throne of England at the age of twenty-
five. As she outlived him by approximately a year and a
half, their lives developed through the same exciting events.
The Queen's views of the changing social and political conditions of her reign have become familiar to everyone conver-
sant with English history. But the views on these same
occurrences in the body politic, such as Lambarde as a learned
lawyer had, have not been exploited at all. Elizabeth's Privy
Councilors had a different stance from Lambarde's for observing and commenting on the times. But from his vantage point
as a historian and magistrate in local government, these events
appeared in a new light. So quite apart from his contributions
as historian and jurist, Lambarde's view of the stirring events
in the reign of Queen Elizabeth I has added a trustworthy
appraisal of Elizabethan England.

Some idea of the motivation for Lambarde's strenuous
activity appears in the preface of his first book, where he

seems compelled to give a reason for his arduous study of Anglo-Saxon manuscripts. He believed, he wrote at that time, that no nation ever succumbed to foreign attack without first having become weak within its own government. This idea recurs in his Charges to the Jurors when he reminds them that they hold within their own hands the power to enforce the laws and maintain the peace of this realm. And he simply practiced what he preached. England was no stronger than the will of the people to work together to achieve order by legal justice. So while Her Majesty and Privy Council contemplated and determined the grand strategy, Lambarde at the grass roots level of Kent tried to make England strong by having the subjects of the Queen recognize the necessity for order. Thus he often appeared to live in two worlds, devoting his privileges and learning to the poor and uneducated, but endeavoring to raise the standards among the country gentry on the commission of the peace. He frequently met apathy in the latter effort, unless some misdemeanor or felony occurred close at home and disturbed the peace of the lord of the manor.

Awards for services rendered came late to Lambarde, not in titles and monopolies or estates but in offices in recognition of his learning and experience. Despite his genius for friendship, apparent in the records of Lincoln's Inn, he went his independent and often lonely way. Yet it can be said of all his honors that he earned them and served well in the various tasks assigned to him, even if he appeared to owe his advancement to high office to a friend who interceded and recommended him. Archbishop Parker was among the churchmen who first advanced his reputation. Although Parker first brought Lambarde to the attention of the powerful Lord Burghley, Lord Cobham later increased Lambarde's prestige by using him so that Lord Burghley appointed him as his deputy in the Alienations Office. Then Sir John Puckering, with whom Lambarde had been called to the bar, appointed him a Master in the Chancery, and another Lincoln's Inn man, Sir Thomas Egerton, on succeeding Puckering as Keeper of the Great Seal, made Lambarde his deputy as Keeper of the Chancery Rolls. Finally Queen Elizabeth I appointed Lambarde Keeper of the Rolls in the Tower of London and asked him to prepare an index of them. Six months later he presented her with this index, *Pandecta Rotulorum*, at a private audience in Greenwich Palace. Two weeks later he died at the age of sixty-five.

Two likenesses of Lambarde appear in the work of George Vertue, the eighteenth-century engraver, who concentrated his attention upon Lambarde's eyes deep set in his sternly molded face. They are confident and sympathetic, firm without being bold, giving a friendly appearance to his handsome face but suggesting a man who could be understanding without yielding his convictions.

Lambarde's scholarly and powerful friends doubtless thought of him as they saw him seated at a desk in his rooms in Lincoln's Inn, his figure silhouetted against the fireplace, candles burning in the silver holders, as he painstakingly worked over his notes from a sheaf of manuscripts before him. Deliberately he would scratch out a word, insert a phrase in his fine script, and scrutinize it. The scene changed through the four ages: the student at work on Anglo-Saxon customs and feudal courts or writing his notes from his peregrinations over Kent; the justice of the peace at work on his manuals and Charges to the Jurors for the administration of the criminal laws; the deputy of the great lords of the realm writing out his reports and histories of office and of the high courts of England; and finally as the Master in the Chancery pondering a case or the contents of a scroll.

To the laborers in the fields, the villagers, and the shopkeepers, however, he was simply "Mr. Justice." As he rode on horseback through the countryside along the narrow lanes, the "handsome man," as he was called, appeared as the symbol of the law. When he stopped to conduct a hearing of alleged criminals and listened to the witnesses, the people observed his patience. They saw his bright eyes, alert and inquisitive. His determinations were based on evidence, not hearsay, and the penalties that he meted out to felons were severe. Or if he bound over a culprit to the next quarter sessions, as was the usual procedure, he took the sureties and proceeded on his way. Yet they trusted him almost as much as they feared him because they regarded him as honest. When the inquiry was over, and he had mounted his horse, they watched him depart. His great outercloak enveloped his body except on a warm summer's day. This cape turned the wind and the rain from him and protected him from the clods of mud from the hooves of passing horses. He soberly acknowledged the heads bowed in respect and the hands raised to the forelocks. He appeared as majestic in the saddle as he did on the bench at the quarter sessions.

William Lambarde's life was characterized by the joy of learning and justice for all. Although he toiled over ancient manuscripts and records, he took his learning into the street, the courtroom, and the privy chamber of his Queen.

Chapter 2

EARLY FAMILY RECORDS
(1536–1556)

William Lambarde was born in the parish of St. Nicholas Acon, London, on October 18, 1536. Within his lifetime the population of London rapidly developed, doubling in size. Even in 1536 the old City was burgeoning forth past its limits, far beyond the old Roman Wall which marked the northern extent in an arc from east to west, from the Tower of London to Blackfriars. The old City was also expanding to the south across the River Thames. In this area known as the Bankside, or Southwark, stood Lambeth Palace, the residence of the Archbishop of Canterbury who had become the titular head of the English church after the Act of Supremacy in 1534, two years before Lambarde's birth, had separated it from Rome. Some forty years later amid the warehouses along the Bankside several of the principal playhouses, such as the Globe Theatre, were to be built. But at this time perhaps the important feature of life in the City itself was its self-government, in which the increasingly prosperous and powerful trade guilds selected two sheriffs and the Lord Mayor for terms of two years from the council of aldermen who served the various wards. This independence of the City in monarchial England may be illustrated by the necessity of the sovereign's gaining permission to enter or pass through the gates and be greeted by the Lord Mayor.

The early records of the Lambarde family are scanty enough, although actually fuller and more complete than those of most Elizabethan families.[1] Since William's father, John Lambarde, rose rapidly in the Drapers' Guild, he also gained riches as a merchant adventurer. The records show how a man with some money in his pocket could come to London from the country and make his fortune during the expanding trade within the City and with ventures across the Channel with the Flemish weavers, if not beyond the seas. John Lambarde's activities have become public record because he held various high offices in the Drapers' Company and also became a member of the Merchant Adventurers' Company.[2] The records of the City show that he served as alderman from two wards and also for a term as sheriff. John Lambarde evidently arrived in the City with funds, since his grandfather was Thomas Lambarde de Ledbury, "*generosus*"; John's father was William de Ledbury, and John named his firstborn after his father. The parish of Ledbury was in Herfordshire, and these manors and farms eventually came to young William Lambarde and were passed on by him to his heir. With these properties intact for six generations, it would seem scarcely idle conjecture that John Lambarde came to London with funds to invest, marry well, and enter politics. For he accumulated a large fortune rather rapidly, probably sustained in the early years and augmented later by his wife's dowry and inheritance. His wife, Juliana, was the daughter and heir of William Horne, reputed to be a rich London merchant.

William's brother, Giles, was born about two years after William, on May 30, 1538; the sister, Anna, was born on April 1, 1540. But apparently Juliana Lambarde did not recover from the illness following the birth of her daughter and she died the following September 20, leaving her husband with three small children ranging in age from four years to five months. She was buried in the church of St. Nicholas Acon, the parish in which her children were born. Anna died within two years.

What happened to William and Giles from the time their mother died until William entered Lincoln's Inn to study law at age twenty, nobody knows. William was eighteen when his father died, and the interval of two years until he was twenty was apparently very important and probably decisive in terms of his development. On the other hand, the record of John Lambarde's life is full and interesting, little as we care about him and much as we should like to know what happened to his sons after the death of his first wife. He married a woman who the records list simply as Alice, careful researcher though William Lambarde himself became in family history. We know something of Alice because she had a daughter by her first marriage. That daughter married Robert Flowers and died before Alice wrote her last will and testament mindful of her son-in-law and grandchild.

Meanwhile John Lambarde's career became spectacular during the reign of young Edward VI, from 1547 to 1553. This was a propitious time for the Protestants because the young King was led to proceed much farther than his father had contemplated progressing in establishing doctrines and revising the Prayer Book. While this religious change affected many persons adversely, it was temporary security for John Lambarde's belief.

He became alderman from Farrington Within from 1547 to 1549 and then evidently moved to Aldersgate, farther east against the old Roman Wall, where he served two terms as alderman, from 1549 to 1554. And it was during this period of representing Aldersgate that he served as one of the two

sheriffs of London from 1552 to 1554.[3] This was a high
honor and, along with his wealth, permitted him to apply for
a coat-of-arms and become a gentleman. It was while he was
sheriff of London, then, that King Edward VI died, and
John Lambarde was among the citizens of London who
signed the King's will.

On this memorable occasion for a commoner, John Lambarde was not only sheriff of London but also Master of
the Drapers' Company, serving as one of its four wardens.
In both politics and trade, he had attained the zenith at this
juncture in his career. Nine days after the death of King
Edward VI, the official description of John Lambarde's coat-
of-arms appeared with the grant on July 15, 1553, as follows:

> Geules a Cheueron vair betwene Thre lambes passant siluer
> Vngled sable; upon his helme on a Torse siluer and geules
> a Trogodises hed Rasy and horned Asur, the mayne porfled
> golde, the eares and Tynes of the hornes siluer, the tongue
> apparante genles manteled asur dobled siluer, as more
> plainly apperith depicted in this margent.[4]

Now John Lambarde contracted to buy the manor known
as Westcombe in East Greenwich, Kent. This manor, adjoined
by Spittle-Combe, had been held from the time of King
Edward II, that is, for more than two hundred years, as a
part of the royal estate of Dartford.[5] Rather close to London,
near Greenwich Palace, where the children of King Henry
VIII were born, this manor represented the desire of the
London merchant for land, as part of the changing social
pattern. There was nothing original about this procedure on
the part of John Lambarde. He was merely following the
particular way of the rich merchants who sought to live
among the peers and the gentry in the country. But these
newly rich men were practical and shrewd; they expected

to gain an income, however small, from their farms. The old county families, the gentry, some of whom in Kent had come from the yeoman, enjoyed country traditions, and their manors and farms provided a way of life and incidentally income. Now the gentry were besieged by two new classes of neighbors, the rich merchants from the city and the former tenant farmers who had saved and borrowed enough money to buy their own land and raise crops for their own purse.

John Lambarde had not ventured far into Kent, but he owned a manor. Then, in the year after the purchase of Westcombe and the granting of his coat-of-arms, John Lambarde died on August 4, 1554. His second wife, Alice, died eight days after her husband, and they were buried near each other in the parish church of St. Michael's.[6] Since the black plague ravished London in that year, and several aldermen were known to have died of the plague, it is highly probable that John and Alice were also victims of this scourge, especially since their deaths occurred within a few days of each other.

John Lambarde left an elaborate will, listing mansions, tenements, messuages (plots of land), warehouses, shops, and a tennis court to Giles Lambarde.[7] Each son received £150. Many of these properties were located across the River Thames, but a few were also within the old City. The extent of these bequests to the younger son indicated not only the great size of John Lambarde's fortune but also his expectation, in the matter of mansions and warehouses, that Giles would carry on the drapery business. Even so, these bequests at this time were particularly unusual for the younger son, for, as Sir Thomas Wilson, himself a younger son, has observed in *The State of England*, printed some forty years later in 1600, the younger son commonly received as his inheritance only what "the catt had left on the malt heap."

Since William was the heir, his share of the estate did not

have to be specified in the will; for example, Westcombe and other properties listed in the Court of Wards as William's inheritance from his father were not itemized in John Lambarde's last will and testament. The heir simply received whatever was not bequeathed to others. But since neither William nor Giles had attained their majorities their inheritance was held in trust for them by the Court of Wards. This court thereon granted to Edmund Hensley, esquire, on August 4, 1554, the custody of William's "body and marriage" as well as all manors, mansions, tenements, messuages, and lands, in London, Kent, and Middlesex. And for this service Edmund Hensley received an annuity of £20, a fee indicative of the value of the estate inherited by William, or in rough approximation in purchasing power of $800 a year. Strikingly enough, the titles of about one third of these properties resided in the possession of the Crown; that is the fee was of the type for service rendered, though the income came to William as it had to his father. In fact when the post mortem of William's property was made many years later, these same properties were listed for him to pass on to his heir.[8]

While the fourteen years after his first wife's death were full of increasing riches and honors for John Lambarde, not one word in these records concerns William and Giles. Where they lived and went to school, who nurtured them in school and church, whom they met and talked with—all these conditions of growing from childhood to young manhood remain unknown. During fourteen years, from the time William Lambarde was four until he became twenty, nothing can be found about his development and education. Nevertheless when he entered Lincoln's Inn, he appeared to be fully prepared as if he, like the majority of his fellows, had received training in either Oxford or Cambridge University. As a matter of fact it was customary for the sons of the gentry and the rich merchants to attend the university before being admitted to one of the four great Inns of Court; only a few attended one of the inferior inns, of which there were several at this time, before entering an Inn of Court.

William Lambarde had an uncle, his mother's brother, who was referred to as a scholar at Oxford. Whether he was a perennial undergraduate, a lecturer, or had merely attended Oxford University, the record did not make clear. But one point is certain: the name of William Lambarde does not appear in the matriculation records of either university. However, that is not overwhelming evidence against his attendance. Unless a young scholar was poor and received stipends listed in the Buttery Book of his college, matriculation for a degree was only essential for a position in the church or in an educational institution. In these years university authorities actually complained that many young scholars in residence had not registered for the degree. Obviously the heirs of rich men had more interest in the practical training provided by the Inns of Court. Legal knowledge was very useful in the managing of estates and business in the changing economic pattern of the time, and so it is not very significant that Lambarde's name did not appear on the university rolls.

Lack of evidence for Lambarde's first-class education before entering Lincoln's Inn cannot be taken as indication of lack of training. On the contrary, it evidently was quite an achievement to gain admittance to one of the Inns of Court, and Lincoln's Inn was certainly prestigious. Perhaps it is merely irritating to be unable to recover where and with whom he received his training. The fact is that he did enter Lincoln's Inn as a highly disciplined young scholar, so proficient in Latin that he immediately became the protégé of several of the most learned men of the time: Matthew Parker, very soon to be the Archbishop of Canterbury; Sir William Cordell, Keeper of the Chancery Rolls, one of the very few Privy Councillors from Mary's reign retained by Elizabeth, though not as a member of her Privy Council; and Laurence Nowell, later Bishop of Litchfield. Since these learned men were reviving information about the Anglo-Saxon language, they would not have welcomed Lambarde to their midst if he had not somewhere demonstrated skill in languages.

Lambarde had somehow discovered the joy of learning and developed the will to seek out the dull and tedious details of matters about which other men wrote and spoke with grace and distinction. But someone had to awaken him, and give him the opportunity to progress in learning, and whoever that person was, he could take satisfaction in the resulting young scholar. Someone had to lead him into the deep religious fervor that characterized him throughout his life. His deep-grained almost fanatical faith in God's providence and laws for mankind had to be first aroused before it could flourish so abundantly that he attracted the attention of churchmen while he was studying the law.

Possibly he owed much to his stepmother, Alice. Or was it Mistress Margaret Bond, his mother's sister? Probably, because of his religious spirit, a parish priest might have been the person under whose tutelage the young Lambarde formed his way of life. In 1546, when Lambarde was ten years old, there were four schools in London, competent to train him well.[9] As early as 1509, John Colet's famous St. Paul's School owed much of its government to the Mercers' Company. St. Paul's School was a model for various schools in which the trade guilds had long taken interest. Nearer his home was the church school of St. Dunstan in the East. The collegiate church of Saint Martin had a first-class school, and there was a fourth school in Bowe Church. The son of John Lambarde could have afforded to attend any school, regardless of the expense.

One might conjecture about the fact that while John Lambarde was Master of the Drapers' Company, the Lord Mayor of London insisted that this worshipful company sponsor at Oxford University the education of two young men from among the apprentices.[10] Surely the dynamic and successful John Lambarde would want his heir to have a gentleman's education. Since his will gave such careful consideration to Giles's future, rather obviously to continue the drapery enterprises, the implication was that John Lambarde did not expect or intend that his heir, William, would follow his father's career in trade. This decision, whether father or son made it, must have been based on some predilection shown by William for scholarship. Nor in retrospect, as one compares Alice Lambarde's will with her husband's, does her influence in this matter appear significant of her interest in her stepsons. She left £20 to each, concerning herself chiefly with provision for her grandchild and her son-in-law, although she was apparently not a wealthy woman. Neither William nor Giles ever in later years evinced any interest in Alice, but both, when they grew to manhood, remembered Mistress Margaret Bond with gratitude.

Even though Mistress Margaret Bond, Juliana Lambarde's sister, had several children, she may have taken her sister's three motherless children into her household. This speculation rests upon two facts. When they grew to manhood both boys remembered her, and Giles entered into partnership with his cousin, Margaret Bond's son. The spirit of gratitude permeating references to Margaret Bond would then indicate perhaps more affection than is usually bestowed upon a well-liked relative.

In retrospect the fullness of the record of John Lambarde's rise in the financial and political affairs of London permits understanding of how his son could present himself to Lincoln's Inn with the kind of preparation granted to only a few young men. There has come down to us no set pattern for the education of rich men's sons in the Elizabethan period. Men like Thomas Egerton and Francis Bacon were tutored at home before being sent to Cambridge University. While John Lambarde's son might be expected to have attended one of the four excellent schools available within the precincts of London, such thinking would be mere speculation.

In looking backwards, nevertheless, fear of speculation need not obliterate facts, in particular about Lambarde's manor in East Greenwich, Kent. There is no evidence to dissuade anyone from assuming that he would have curiosity about his property, particularly an estate recently acquired by his father shortly before death. The physical fitness that made possible his exploration of Kent did not have to be acquired on the playing fields of Eton, or during vacation jaunts between terms at the university, or wherever he might have been studying. It would be less reasonable to think that a city-bred boy should suddenly wish to spend long days in the mist and sun in remote areas, finding his way through forests and around swamps and up and down hills. On the contrary, a studious boy might even wish to do these things but lack the stamina and experience to carry out his wishes.

Hence the assumption must be made that during these years Lambarde began the rugged outdoor life that in later years became a matter of record.

Chapter 3

AT LINCOLN'S INN AND
ARCHAIONOMIA (1556–1569)

Even while his property remained in the custody of the
Court of Wards, William Lambarde was admitted to Lincoln's Inn on August 15, 1556, to study the law.[1] And here
began the major influences and experiences that were recognizable throughout his entire life. It was at Lincoln's Inn
that he formed the friendships that accounted for the awards
given him; there under extraordinary circumstances he
formed his own philosophy of the law and its administration; he also gained some experience as a Member of Parliament; but most important of all, he there compiled his
first book.

Lincoln's Inn was one of the four Inns of Court; the
others were Gray's Inn, the Inner Temple, and the Middle
Temple. These were residential establishments with distinguished traditions dating from ancient times. In the beginning these societies were instituted for the sons of the nobility
to acquire the learning necessary for statecraft and the
management of their feudal domains, as the lords of the
manors held feudal courts to hear and determine grievances
among their people to punish those who broke the customs

and laws. The objective then was practical learning and continued to remain so in Lambarde's time. The principal change was in the kind of students that were admitted to these traditional halls and residences. Amidst these changing social conditions, the sons of merchants and farmers were admitted now to these societies formerly restricted to the scions of the peers and the gentry. Londoners referred to the Inns as the Third University.[2]

The students in these Inns of Court had to pay for their own maintenance, which was costly, and the normal period of preparation for being called to the bar was seven years, in contrast to the three years required for the baccalaureate degree in the universities. Unlike students in the universities who were poor, and consequently received stipends from various trust funds, young men without sufficient means to meet the obligations of the Inns of Court had to attend one of the inferior inns.

The four Inns of Court were located in the West End of London from Fleet Street to Holborn. The Inner Temple and the Middle Temple were in Fleet Street, Lincoln's Inn in Chancery Lane, and Gray's Inn in Holborn, with trees and open fields beyond, not tightly packed together as they appear with elaborate additions today. Within the gates of the old courts were trees and gardens, providing a pleasant view from the residence halls. Each Inn had its great hall and library in which the amenities of the contemplative life were maintained. Beyond these ancient quadrangles were fields.

The inferior inns, situated nearby, did not have the privilege of calling students to the bar. In particular, were two Sergeant's Inns, one in Fleet Street and the other in Chancery Lane, both at this time chiefly residential. They too provided Readers and limited training, as did Clifford's Inn, New Inn, Lion's Inn, and Clement's Inn. Those familiar with Shakespeare's *King Henry IV, Part II* will recall the silly old justices, Shallow and Silence, who reminded Falstaff of their gay and roistering days in London at Clement's Inn. The men of the Inns of Court, who attended the public playhouses as well as fostering the presentation of plays on festive occasions, thus had an opportunity to laugh heartily at these justices of the peace who were allegedly trained in Clement's Inn. Hence Shakespeare's satire on the justices of the peace does emphasize how necessary was Lambarde's work in standardizing this office and raising the requirements, two developments that Elizabeth herself then recognized and made operative in the Commission of the Peace.

But when Lambarde entered Lincoln's Inn in 1556, Queen Mary had two more years to rule and was also facing the most difficult prospects with the return of her royal husband to Spain. Nominal Anglicans had become Roman Catholics again, but the seeds of the reformation had matured and consequently persons with convictions had to suffer whether they were Protestants or not. On the other hand, the Roman Catholics who had steadfastly maintained their faith, in particular many of the great peers who had retained their priests to chant the oratories in private chapels, now had hope for security. But Mary's alliance with King Philip II was an unsettling marriage, despite her firm position about religion.

In Lambarde's time the Inns of Court provided sanctuary as well as the fellowship of kindred minds, even if none of the Protestants could look forward to preferment at court as a Privy Councillor, ambassador, or judge in any jurisdiction. For the young man interested in statecraft with his eyes fixed upon high office, these conditions were tantamount to tragic isolation. To rise someday to be Attorney General, then Solicitor General, and Lord Keeper of the Great Seal or Lord Chancellor required patience enough, but if no rules of strategy obtained as a result of shifting religious doctrines and alliances, the future offered no hope of preferment.

After adjustment to twenty years and more of nominal Protestantism, a readjustment to Roman Catholicism affected an ambitious man's appetite as well as his soul.

The Four Inns of Court were rivals for the appointments to high office, but at this time Lincoln's Inn and Gray's Inn were particularly fortunate in perpetuating their men in coveted positions. If money was requisite for admission to the bar, then advancement depended upon talent and ingenuity in walking the tightrope to royal favor.

The house, as an Inn of Court was called by its members, gained its distinction not only from its men in high office but also from the quality of the outerbarristers, benchers, and lawyers in residence, for after being called to the bar, a member continued to reside in the house and identified himself with it by signing his legal papers, for example, "William Lambarde of Lincoln's Inn." Of course he did not have to live in his rooms, though they were available to him throughout his life as his official residence.

Discipline was strict. The Council, composed of benchers and barristers, dictated the standards to which the students conformed. They read old Year Books, the printing of which was discontinued at this time, Magna Charta, surveys by great judges such as Glanville, Bracton, and Fortesque, but in particular they scrutinized famous cases and studied the ordinances and statutes. They depended upon the exposition of certain statutes by a Reader and the practical experience gained in their moot courts. On the one hand was the revived interest in Anglo-Saxon customs and laws, and on the other hand the Roman laws which undergirded the ecclesiastical courts. These were the two extremes, but in between were the established customs and precedents which were the significant part of the great unwritten law called natural law. The joy of learning was not to be shared by all, but the few found opportunity for broad reading and speculation. Such was the appeal for a man like young Lambarde. He could follow his flair for language and take his time about pursuing the narrower course of study.

In Elizabethan England the community of scholars was so incredibly small that each one became recognized for his individual specialty. Lambarde's skill with Latin brought him to the attention of Laurence Nowell, who was occupying his brother's rooms in Lincoln's Inn, seeking seclusion during Queen Mary's scourge of Protestant divines and devoting his time to the collection and translation of Anglo-Saxon manuscripts. Matthew Parker, the leader of this movement, who was also in seclusion, sought to recover ancient rules and traditional interpretations given by very early leaders of the church in Britain. His broad learning thus was forming the background from which he could emerge a few years later to assume, under Queen Elizabeth, the highest office in the English church. Lambarde's destiny, then, was formed in part by his being a Protestant at a significant time for study.

Under Laurence Nowell's guidance Lambarde began to assist with the making of glossaries and determining rules of grammar for this ancient language. He participated in the deciphering of words and phrases from the Anglo-Saxon manuscripts collected by Nowell and then in the determination of priority among these ancient scripts. This was a painful and slow way to prepare oneself for being called to the bar.

Only scraps of minimal information about the common law came to Lambarde. On the other hand, the revelation of ecclesiastical polity revealed in these manuscripts was useful to churchmen. But the important discovery that Lambarde made was that he liked this sort of work. He gave himself to it with such care that Nowell eventually gave him the manuscripts and all his own work for Lambarde to carry on, and

Lambarde eventually made this research into his first book, *Archaionomia*.

This association with Laurence Nowell, who later became the Bishop of Litchfield, and with his brother Alexander, later the Dean of St. Paul's, whose preaching aroused Elizabeth's ire more often than her approval, was propitious for a young man seeking his future in the church.[3] Certainly Matthew Parker's friendship was worth the student lawyer's sacrifice of progress toward the bar. But these men, useful in helping him to become known as a scholar, were aiding him to discover his lifelong interest in manuscripts. His forte was here, rather than in the courtroom.

Probably it was during these years that Lambarde learned to control his longing for the strenuous life of the man of action and to devote concentrated scholarly attention to meticulous tasks. This remarkable achievement was recognized by Laurence Nowell, who decided to supply him with rare manuscripts and encourage him to complete the exacting and arduous project of translating the Anglo-Saxon scripts into Latin.

There was early recognition of Lambarde's administrative ability in managing social affairs, for his name appeared more frequently in the records of Lincoln's Inn than that of any other young man during these years, as in charge of various important matters such as the Reader's Dinner. (Each year between terms an eminent person—a learned judge or scholarly barrister—was presented by the Council of the Society to explicate the text of an important statute, usually one of recent enactment and consequence. The learned man's interpretation of the implications of the statute was then followed by a period of discussion, during which bright and perceptive students arose and asked questions. This discussion period sometimes resulted in debate, although more often, the debate ensued in a later meeting of their own moot courts.)

The students also had their Revels, festive dinners and dances. In later years the students at Gray's Inn, the Middle Temple, and the Inner Temple presented plays on these festive occasions, but during Lambarde's time in Lincoln's Inn not much attention was paid to presenting plays. The so-called first theater had yet to be built in Finnsbury Fields north of London. So accounts of the Inns of Court men attending the public playhouses belong to a later era also. Now there were just festive dinners and dances.

Lambarde evidently believed that he was being used too much as steward, for he paid a fine for refusing to be steward, as did his friend John Puckering. Puckering was called to the bar at the same time as Lambarde and years later was to reach the zenith as Lord Keeper of the Great Seal, at which time he appointed Lambarde a Master in the great prerogative Court of Chancery.[4] Another friend of these years was Thomas Egerton, a few years younger than Lambarde, who after a brilliant career at the bar became Attorney General and Solicitor General. He attained the office of Lord Keeper of the Seal under Queen Elizabeth and created Lambarde Keeper of the Rolls in the Chancery; under King James I, Egerton became Lord Chancellor and the recipient of other honors.[5]

Both Puckering and Egerton evinced very early their abilities to be leaders of men. But the records of Lincoln's Inn present no more evidence of their attainments than of Lambarde's. One cannot avoid the impression that Lambarde as a young man appeared marked for greatness. The fact that he was called upon to arrange and direct many social events would suggest that he was well graced in presence and general appearance, as would the legend that he was called the "handsome man of Kent."

His friendships appeared to be far ranging: the rich and less well-to-do, the intellectual and the unambitious. None among the rich and brilliant was closer to him than Ralph Rokeby, who had already begun to earn distinction for establishing English legal procedures in the law courts of Ireland.[6] Later, when he returned home, he became Master of the High Court of Requests. While in this office, he seemed to be responsible for having Lambarde appointed by the Privy Council to serve on several commissions. He revealed his high respect for Lambarde's integrity and knowledge of the law by designating Lambarde to be co-executor, with Sir Thomas Egerton, of his estate. Since his bequests were detailed and complicated, Lambarde had the work to do at that time. But now in Lincoln's Inn the bonds of this lifelong friendship were formed.

Lambarde established another enduring friendship at this time with Humphrey Windham, who was evidently not an ambitious man.[7] Lambarde in later years referred to Windham as "my bedfellow in Lincoln's Inn." After Lambarde's brother died, Windham married his widow, and Lambarde apparently was the matchmaker. Although his association with his brother was tenuous, Lambarde continued to admire Giles's wife, Margery, and in this instance he brought his two friends together. When years later he made his own will, he entrusted Windham and Margery with the special care of his children, an indication of his sustained friendship and confidence in their judgments.

Early friendships apparently continued to remain thus mutually respected through these crucial years of change in the social life of England. Though of course the eligible group was particularly small by modern standards, the story of Lambarde's life depends upon his holding close these persons that he met in his days at Lincoln's Inn.

William Sedley, the scion of an aristocratic Kentish family and a man who improved his social position and increased his wealth by marriage, became a collector of fine books which he shared with and also gave to Lambarde.[8] He too made use of Lambarde's skill as a lawyer, but this friendship apparently was based on books and learning, a mutuality of interests. On the other hand, like Humphrey Windham, Sedley evinced no soaring ambition or burning desire to grasp power or assume responsibility for public service. Both these men lived quietly and well, occupying their days with extensive reading and shrewd management of their estates.

These five men in Lincoln's Inn were approximately Lambarde's age, either a few years younger or older. But their varied interests and careers were being formed, as were Lambarde's complex activities, during those student days. The notable feature of these friendships, as they developed in later years, was the mutual respect they all held for one another. Doubtless Lambarde made other friendships among his contemporaries, but these particular ones endured.

During these years Lambarde attended the Second Parliament as a Duchy Nominee and all but ruined his career. As a matter of fact, it must be remembered that Queen Elizabeth called Parliament only ten times in her long reign of forty-four years. Usually the Parliament was called for a term of a few weeks, the longest session lasting less than six months. So it is obvious that being a Member of Parliament in Elizabeth's time was scarcely a career. Ever since Elizabeth's ascension the Lords and Members of Parliament alike had worried over the succession to the throne of their virgin Queen. Her marriage had become the major concern of her government, and she made the most of it, seeming about to make her choice of husband, and thus with the expectation of an heir, to resolve the anxiety. But while she delayed her decision, the two powerful factions, Stuart and Suffolk, sought recognition as the true successor should she default.

Elizabeth had much to gain by delay, since she could temporize with the great powers on the Continent and avoid war, while seeming to be on the verge of wedding a foreign prince. She herself declared that she had married England, but her subjects awaited her marriage and subsequent motherhood. Yet now she had ruled for five years without either marrying or designating whether the Stuart or the Suffolk line would succeed her.

Lambarde attended the session of the Second Parliament called on January 12, 1563. This Parliament was prorogued on April 10, 1563, and resumed on September 13, 1563. The Members were restive and had requested that Her Majesty inform them of her intentions, or at least designate the line of succession. Lord Burghley read her reply, in which she declined to reveal either her plans for marriage or to indicate her choice between the contending houses. And there was no applause when Burghley finished reading this message. The Members of Parliament were not only disgruntled but expressed their views with acerbity. On the other hand, the Stuart and Suffolk factions remained quiet, not wishing to disturb the delicate balance or to incur the Queen's displeasure while both could still retain hope.

Three days later Lambarde arose and declared that the Queen had made a grave error in avoiding the issue. Surely it was her duty to quiet the fears and unrest of her subjects. He argued learnedly that the welfare of her government required that her decision be made. Even though he presented learned precedents and spoke in good faith, his speech seemed audacious. He was only a young law student, speaking his mind, and however forthright, honest, and necessary was his speech, he had challenged authority.[9] He then returned to Lincoln's Inn to manage the annual Revels held on All Saints' Day.[10] But it would seem in retrospect that he had committed an unpardonable blunder in diplomacy. More than that, he had revealed the uncompromising characteristic that was to appear again and again in his complex nature; namely, to speak the truth at all costs.

Now he settled down again to the time-consuming work on Nowell's Anglo-Saxon manuscripts, which seemed to have become more important to him than being called to the bar. He acquired books on agriculture, Latin treatises which he underscored and marked with cross-references in the margins. He also bought books on the Roman law. His reading seems to have been far in excess of that required. And so he lingered on in Lincoln's Inn past the seven years that students usually resided there before being admitted to the bar.

He was called to the bar, with John Puckering, on June 13, 1567, almost eleven years after the date of his admission to Lincoln's Inn.[11] The next year his first book, *Archaionomia*, was printed in London by John Day, a well-known printer of books by Protestant divines. This book was a compilation of the Anglo-Saxon customs and ecclesiastical laws derived from the manuscripts given him years before by Laurence Nowell. On one page appeared the Anglo-Saxon text and on the opposite page Lambarde's Latin translation, so that both lawyers and clergymen interested in these ecclesiastical laws could readily scan them in the Latin translation.

In the dedication of this book to Sir William Cordell, Lambarde also gave lavish acknowledgment to Laurence Nowell and Archbishop Parker. To these three men he owed, he wrote, a great debt for assistance. He also stated his reasons for presenting this book, paraphrasing certain well-known classical thinkers about the law. "No nation was ever conquered that had not first suffered disorder from its enemies within." He then explained, also in Latin, that the laws of England were "like a wall built of stone and oak to defend a city." He advocated that severe penalties be given to persons disobeying the law, so that through fear the people would learn to respect the law. He based this thought on the premise that authority was vested in the sovereign, but ultimately the maintenance of order derived from the people themselves.

This was not precisely a young man's book. Since he was now thirty-two and widely read, it is not at all surprising that these ideas were repeated by him later in life, particularly in his Charges to the Jurors at the quarter sessions in Maidstone, the county town in Kent, and on various commissions.

The reception of *Archaionomia*, in the tenth year of the reign of Queen Elizabeth, could almost have been predicted with certainty because of the eminence of the persons named in the Dedication, or "Epistola." As Matthew Parker, now the powerful head of the church of England as the Archbishop of Canterbury, had contributed his scholarship to Lambarde's book, the authority of office as well as of recognized learning assured the purchasers of *Archaionomia* that the leader of the revival of Anglo-Saxon studies favored the book. Laurence Nowell, with whose manuscripts and studies this work had begun, had become the Dean of Litchfield. Sir William Cordell was soon to become the Governor of Lincoln's Inn, where as early as 1553 and 1554 he had served as the Lenten Reader. Lambarde praised Cordell, Nowell, and Parker for their counsel and assistance so much that his own hard work seemed representative of a cooperative enterprise.

John Foxe, a member of the exclusive circle of divines and scholars headed by Archbishop Parker, had had acclaim as the author of the *Book of Martyrs* (*The Acts and Monuments*, London: John Day, 1563), a book still famous and respected; and he evidently was so pleased with *Archaionomia* that he sent a copy of it to William Bradbridge, then the Dean of Salisbury and later Bishop of Exeter. Foxe wrote on the flyleaf of this copy that the author was known to them both as a person with magnificent learning in languages in addition to his many other talents: *"Vir, multis et egregiis dotibus ornatissimus Gulielmus Lambardus, is ipse qui superiores tuas de me literas."* [12] Such praise from the author of a distinguished book indicated that Lambarde had acquired a reputation for skill in languages before his *Archaionomia* was printed. Moreover, Lambarde had to have vast learning in the law and its procedures, in addition to skill in languages, in order to make sense of the unfamiliar forms in the Anglo-Saxon script.

The copy of *Archaionomia* that Foxe sent to Bradbridge became a part of the Bridgewater collection of books associated with Thomas Egerton. But in 1568, Thomas Egerton was residing as a student in Lincoln's Inn and had not yet been called to the bar to begin his illustrious career under both Elizabeth and James I. A copy of *Archaionomia* in the Folger Shakespeare Library has the signature of William Shakespeare, believed by many scholars to be authentic. This is significant, as Shakespeare was not born until 1564 and thus was only four years old when *Archaionomia* was printed. This book apparently continued in esteem for many years, or why would Shakespeare have acquired it? But no arguments need to be advanced to support the continued use of this book even after the death of Lambarde, since the common lawyers in the seventeenth century avidly searched it for precedents which they evidently highly esteemed. On the other hand, twentieth-century scholars in the fields of Anglo-Saxon, paleography, and history have pointed out certain inaccuracies in selecting primary texts, misunderstanding of Anglo-Saxon words and syntax, and in general have warned against the use of this book because of these matters unknown to Lambarde and his learned associates.[13] Yet it would seem to an outsider that the historians who have condemned a few items in this book might also have recognized the significance of its reception, use, and influence some three hundred years ago, when it was a veritable landmark on an uncharted road to Old English learning.

In addition to indicating the kind of sponsorship or patronage that Lambarde was enjoying in 1568, *Archaionomia* presented a writer concerned with Kentish antiquities. And this latter fact was indeed significant, for the man who owned a manor and farms in Kent now also appeared to be ready to practice his profession in Kent. Certainly no other lawyer knew as much about Kentish laws as did Lambarde. And when the title to a tract of land began with the listings recorded in the *Domesday Book,* knowledge of the procedures of the ecclesiastical and feudal courts would, to say the least, be useful if not decisive in the handling of conveyances and mortgages of property. The interest of the author of *Archaionomia* then seemed to turn from legal matters to antiquarian studies of the topography of Kent, ancient Roman camps and towns, roads, bridges, and the activities of Kentish people from ancient times to his own. His concern with the law became secondary, even though his signature appears on extant legal writs, conveyances, and contracts in both the public domain and privately held papers.

There can be no doubt that Lambarde was surveying Kent and taking copious notes on what he saw even before the printing of *Archaionomia.* With the patronage he had acquired, as well as in his own right, he had the opportunity to make new friends within the closed circle of the county families. He then spent the following years of his life, from the age of thirty-two until after he celebrated his forty-fourth birthday, satisfying this abounding curiosity about Kentish persons and places. His life as a jurist and author of important books on legal procedures and the high courts of England all came into his life after he was in middle age.

Chapter 4

"THE PERAMBULATOR" AND ARCHBISHOP PARKER
(1570–1580)

Within two years after the printing of his *Archaionomia*, Lambarde finished the manuscript of his second book, *A Perambulation of Kent*. However this date is confusing because this original manuscript was later revised, and the book was not printed until 1576. Probably it then seemed to Lambarde that his years of work on this manuscript had finally ended, since he had done more work than possibly could have been crammed into the two years intervening between the printing of *Archaionomia* and this manuscript of *A Perambulation of Kent*, which he finished when he was thirty-four.

Kent was an ideal county for a topographer and historian to explore and write about. The battleground of the ancient Jutes, Kent was one of the states in the Anglo-Saxon Heptarchy from the fifth century, though historians seem to differ on the conquest of Hengist and Horsa in 449. The Roman Catholic mission of St. Augustine of Canterbury came to Aethelbert as early as 597. So in Kent there were numerous religious shrines and houses, ancient Roman camps and towns, all of great interest to a young man who was translating ancient customs and laws from the Anglo-Saxon manuscripts. In most likelihood, therefore, *Archaionomia* and *A Perambulation of Kent* progressed hand in hand.

Kent was then, and is still, one of the most beautiful counties in England. From the white cliffs of Dover to the great Weald, fields of grain, hops, and rich meadows for cattle and sheep give Kent the appearance of a garden. The rich soil lies in the middle. The chalk land runs east to west in the north, but south of this narrow strip lie fertile fields and forests, particularly east and west of the Medway River. Both the Stour River and the Darent River are important, but the Medway flows northward through the area where long ago Lambarde spent many years of hard work. Of course his own manor of Westcombe was in the northwest corner, but he spent most of his life in the rural area and towns near to and along the Medway River.

Kent was the spawning grounds for independent leaders of rebellions, fighters for freedom who were not always understood and admired. Yet to name Wat Tyler, Jack Cade, and Sir Thomas Wyatt reminds us that from the fourteenth century to the Spanish marriage of Queen Mary in the middle of the sixteenth century, Kentish men had no hesitancy in declaring their opinions, despite a stern monarchy, long in advance of the dawning of democracy in England. Whether the cause was wages, misrule, or a foreign marriage, these men led stouthearted fellows into London to force their opinions on the government, and suffered death as a result of their efforts.

Lambarde believed that the sturdy independence of the Kentish yeoman developed from the ancient division of property among all the children, known as gavelkind. It was in contrast to primogeniture, or inheritance by the heir, or oldest child. Gavelkind was peculiar to Kent, though it was known and practiced occasionally in other counties. Lambarde's view was that when men owned their own land, instead of leasing from the oldest brother, they did not meekly accept injustice. They were not in awe of authority and power.

Very early in his survey of Kent Lambarde made a map of the county, his "Carde of the Shyre," indicating the courses of the three principal rivers, the chalk downs in the north, the great Weald, the principal hills, forests, and the verdant valleys. Then he noted the sites of ancient Roman camps and towns, Henry VIII's castles, and particularly the beacons that warned mariners of rocks and also guided sea captains in approaching the Cinque Ports. This old French description of the five main ports to Kent and Sussex originally included Hastings, Romney, Hythe, Dover, and Sandwich, but Rye and Winchelsea were added later, though the term remained in use.

The Cinque Ports had special tax privileges and more independence than other towns, but they also had responsibilities and expenses that balanced the benefits they received. During Lambarde's time, Lord Cobham, the Lord Lieutenant of the Shire, was also the Lord Warden of the Cinque Ports, an important duty then, though in later times an honorary title of distinction. Dover was the chief port, the gateway to the Continent, on the old Roman Road from London past Greenwich and Rochester. This was the highway, the old Watling Street Road, along which the seafaring men came to London. It was the road followed by scions of wealthy families on their way to the grand tour of Europe. Here loitered the homeless men, the cutpurses and wenchers. And this was the entrance to England for the royal princes and ambassadors.

Lambarde's interests were inclusive: geological formations, trees, flowers, birds, and bees. He was interested in stone quarries, sand, and marshes, like Romney Marsh. He explained certain words in common usage: for example, *borse*, familiar in *borsholder*, as signifying a pledge or surety; in other counties the Kentish term *borsholder* was replaced by *tithingman*, signifying a person in charge of ten others. He described the division of Kent into *lathes* which are subdivided into *hundreds*. These word lists indicated his continued interest in language already exhibited in *Archaionomia*.

Lambarde's knowledge of basic customs and laws enabled him to explain such procedures as the *court baron*, in which the lord of the manor heard and determined grievances among his people sometimes as often as every three weeks. The *court leet* was usually held twice a year and provided an opportunity for the selection of certain local officers in the parish. The *frank-pledge*, an oath of allegiance, was made at the *court leet*. He presented his learning about these local matters in a readable style acceptable to scholars as well as to the gentry and yeomen. Despite the formidable array of knowledge, he seemed to be trying to interest all Kentish men who could read.

The advice and influence of Archbishop Parker was at this time very great in directing Lambarde's work. Parker was sixty-six years old and venerable in the councils of Queen Elizabeth. So if Lambarde required any motivation or encouragement to continue his antiquarian studies after *Archaionomia*, Parker's influence must be considered. On the other hand, Lambarde's insatiable curiosity about Kentish lore probably needed no stimulation, since he had demonstrated that he had the leisure and sufficient income to indulge in his private studies rather than to engage in the practice of the law. The inclusiveness of the material in this manuscript of his survey of Kent would indicate, however, that more than two years of diligent searching and writing of segments of it preceded its completion. He had sustained his interest long enough to write the first county history of England.

Did Parker introduce Lambarde to Thomas Wotton and suggest that the manuscript be sent to him? Thomas Wotton was the man most competent to examine this manuscript, for he himself had made an avocation of Kentish lore, and he doubtless had become involved in Lambarde's inquiries rather early.[1] Perhaps *Archaionomia* was sufficient to interest Wotton in Lambarde. Probably Parker had interceded in Lambarde's behalf. But this survey of Kentish antiquities would by its very nature be an enterprise of interest to him. Whatever the means of association, Lambarde sent Wotton the manuscript for his perusal, suggestions, and correction of errors.

Thomas Wotton was fifteen years older than Lambarde, and of distinguished lineage. An ancestor, Sir Nicholas Wotton, had served as Lord Mayor of London as early as 1416, and again in 1431. Thomas had been confined to the Tower of London during the reign of Queen Mary, but aside from the threat of losing his head, he had survived that ordeal. Queen Elizabeth had asked him to be one of her Privy Councillors, but he had graciously explained that he would serve her as High Sheriff of Kent during her first year of rule, an office then tantamount to the later office of Lord Lieutenant; whereupon he then retired to his beautiful estate at Boughton Malherbe, preferring to tend his garden rather than be of the Privy Council.

The Queen regarded Wotton with great respect and sought his views, for he had a way of looking at problems and life in general quite different from that of any of her courtiers. He was humble but aristocratic, a true gentleman amidst a hoard of self-seekers. His gentle nature and love of Kent set him apart from other men as a person the Queen could trust. Wotton interceded for persons in need of justice.

He wrote wise letters to relatives and friends. He zealously represented Kent and thus became a veritable symbol of Kentish independence in a quiet but firm way.

After delivering his manuscript to Thomas Wotton, Lambarde was now ready to settle down and look to his domestic life. Perhaps it was inevitable that his inquiries made among the gentry and yeomen in Kent should lead to his establishing a large acquaintanceship during this period. When, for example, he visited the site of the old Roman camp near Wrotham, he found himself at Ightham Common. To the north of this site and west of Wrotham he came to the manor of St. Cleres, Ightham, which had a long history from the time of King Richard I. It had belonged to Sir Thomas Boleyn, the father of Anne, the wife of King Henry VIII and mother of Queen Elizabeth. Now it was owned by George Multon, a justice of the peace and a gentleman who had risen from independent yeoman stock by careful management of his farms. George Multon had purchased the manor of St. Cleres from Richard Farmer, after alienating his manor of Aldham and other lands in East Peckham to Thomas Polhill. At that time, Multon was residing in East Peckham and had followed a long line of yeomen. Now at seventy-one, he was the father of relatively young children, a son, also named George, and a daughter, Jane, who was then sixteen, but soon to celebrate her seventeenth birthday.[2]

Lambarde was thirty-four and certainly an eligible bachelor. Moreover, he was evidently a lonely man who paradoxically had many influential friends and acquaintances and yet few homes into which he could enter informally. So if the Multons opened their home to him, and George Multon treated him as his son, Lambarde would readily find a new experience in the family life at St. Cleres, Ightham.

If their friendship began early, then Lambarde had observed Jane as she grew to womanhood. And now she was sixteen, the age when girls married in Elizabethan England. Though Lambarde was twice her age, he proposed to her and gained her father's consent. With his reputation for being handsome, this rich, young scholar might have married a wealthy widow and progressed in court circles. Romantic marriages for love were at this time contracted by the poor and the extremely prosperous. Lambarde's lack of social ambition and independence of nature would account for his interest in Jane, who for all we know may well have been a highly desirable girl. On the other hand, he apparently was residing with the Multons at this time and not at Westcombe. And after his marriage to Jane, on September 11, 1570, shortly before her seventeenth birthday, the young couple continued to live at St. Cleres.

The usual marriage contract, such as that between young George Multon and his wife, Audrey, at a later date, has not been found for Lambarde and Jane. But evidently a marriage contract existed, for years later Lambarde released his moiety in St. Cleres. Multon had received from Queen Elizabeth "demesne lands," held outright in fee simple, as well as other farms. So Multon was well-to-do and doubtless gave his only daughter a proper dowry. But since the Lambardes continued to reside in St. Cleres, the old saying that the father had not lost a daughter but gained a son was literally true in this instance; indeed, the friendship between father and son-in-law continued to develop.

Lambarde now projected a survey of England after the manner of his *A Perambulation of Kent,* the manuscript of which Thomas Wotton was now perusing. No letters between Wotton and Lambarde have come to light, but quite probably they conversed during this period, as only a short day's horseback ride separated them. Some months later Wotton forwarded the manuscript of Lambarde's survey of Kent to Archbishop Parker. Meanwhile Lambarde was reading manuscripts in the library of Rochester Cathedral, where he found a manuscript unknown to Archbishop Parker. While Parker was reading *A Perambulation of Kent,* Lambarde continued to seek more information and share his findings with his patron.

In the spring of 1573, before the beginning of the Lenten season, Parker entertained Queen Elizabeth in Lambeth Palace, the chief residence of the Archbishop of Canterbury. He was conscious of his failing health and he planned this tribute to her Majesty as rather a farewell gesture of gratitude, sparing no pains in devising music and pageantry suitable to the occasion; for he had ruled over her spiritual domain in a critical time with patience and wisdom, much as Lord Treasurer Burghley had in administering temporal matters. Choirs of sweet music, tableaux, and rare food and old wines revealed his thoughtfulness as the Prince of her Church. But what was most important for Lambarde was Parker's endeavor to bring the antiquarian to her attention. Evidently Parker believed that Elizabeth should recognize Lambarde's scholarship, for immediately thereafter a special privilege was granted to Lambarde.

When the Queen left Lambeth for Greenwich Palace, she began the observance of Lent with a rededication of herself to God in a service that Lambarde was permitted to witness and record. She observed Maundy Thursday with great humility in Greenwich Palace, where she had been born thirty-nine years before. She arranged to perform the remarkable ceremony of penitence by reenacting the rite instituted by Jesus Christ, namely, washing the feet of the poor and giving alms to them in observance of the Saviour's humility.

Lambarde was not a clergyman. Nor was he a favorite of the Queen. He was an outsider. Without doubt any privilege accorded him could only have come from the intercession of Archbishop Parker with Her Majesty. Something of consequence for Lambarde's future must have been in the great prelate's mind. And Lambarde described the entire proceedings with reverence and understanding.[3]

Lambarde began his record of this symbolic ceremony with a description of how the great hall of the palace was decorated for the occasion. The high table was prepared with surrounding cushions and rugs, and down the length of the hall seats were arranged for the poor women, amidst other carpets and cushions. Thirty-nine poor women, representing the Queen's age, were ushered in and seated. Next the Yeoman of the Laundry appeared with grooms carrying basins of holy water and clean towels. He then proceeded to wash the feet of the poor women with the warm water scented with flowers. In each case he made the sign of the cross and then kissed the feet just above the toes. The Almoner appeared and repeated the same ceremony. Finally the Queen herself entered the great hall, followed by thirty-nine ladies of her court. Her Majesty then performed the ceremony already conducted by the Yeoman of the Laundry and her Almoner: she washed the feet, made the sign of the cross, and kissed the feet of each of the poor women. When she had finished, she gave to each woman a purse containing twenty shillings. Her gift of alms was thus in lieu, Lambarde explained, of the ancient custom of redeeming Her Majesty's gown. Queen Elizabeth then took her royal seat of state and listened to the singing of the choir, after which she withdrew from the hall.

Lambarde was apparently much moved by this ceremony and described it in the most lucid prose that he ever wrote. With mellowness of style, this essay reveals his apparent endeavor to preserve the details of this long ceremony in a historic document. Such attention to details, though characteristic of Lambarde's manner of writing, perhaps needed no prompting from Archbishop Parker, but it appears to be more than careful recording of an event. If it was intended for Queen Elizabeth's reading and preservation among her state papers, it was appropriately prepared. Yet he gained nothing as a result of it.

Parker's careful studying of Lambarde's *A Perambulation of Kent* led to his insistence that Lambarde insert a passage from his own study of the work and precepts of Lanfranc, the eleventh-century head of the church, dealing with the interpretation of both the Old and New Testaments of the Bible. Parker had published several months earlier some of his findings in *De Antiquitate Britannicae Ecclesiae Cantauriensis*. . . . Here is the insertion that Parker suggested:

> Quando Willielmus Rex gloriosus morabatur in Normannia, Lanfrancus erat princeps & custos Angliae, subjectis sibi omnibus principibus & juvantibus in nis quae ad defensionem vel pacem pertinebant regni secundum leges patriae; Lectioni affiduas & ante episcopatum & episcopatu quanto poterat,—Et quia scripturae, scriptorum vitio, erant nimium corruptae, omnes, tam veteris quam novi Testamenti Libros, nec non etiam scripta sanctorum, saera secundum orthodoxam sedem studuit corrigere.[4]

Meanwhile Lambarde himself had come upon an important manuscript in the library of the Priory of St. Andrew in Rochester, Kent. This manuscript was called the *Textus Roffensis*, and apparently was unknown to both Archbishop Parker and Laurence Nowell when Lambarde discovered it. Yet it contained several important statements about ancient ecclesiastical laws and courts, which belonged with those printed by Lambarde in *Archaionomia*. In general, however, there were many miscellaneous items concerning the rights and possessions of the See of Rochester and the Church of St. Andrew. Genealogies of the Saxon kings in Kent and

Wessex were in this manuscript, as well as the oaths and ordeals prescribed in those Anglo-Saxon times.

This discovery was much appreciated by Archbishop Parker, and he urged Lambarde to include selections from this material in *A Perambulation of Kent*. Though more than two years had passed since Lambarde believed that he had finished his book and sent it off to Wotton, he was now engaged in amplifying it and revising certain parts of it.

By May 9, 1573, the various additions and corrections had apparently been made, for on that date Parker wrote to Lord Burghley and mentioned Lambarde's manuscript, offering to forward it to Burghley. He referred to Lambarde as "an honest and learned observer," and explained that he had received this manuscript because the author wanted his friends "to peruse, to correct, and amend" it before he gave further effort to it and had it printed.[5] Hence it would seem that Parker was calling Burghley's attention to a person that the great man did not know. If so, then Lambarde was in the enviable position of having the two most powerful statesmen in the realm review his manuscript. He was fortunate to have Parker bring him and his work to the attention of the great Lord Burghley, especially if Parker had in mind an office for him.

Later in the year, on June 27, 1573, Parker again had reason to write to Burghley and again, incidentally, mentioned Lambarde's manuscript.[6] This time he forwarded Lambarde's Preface and indicated that it was the author's intention to dedicate his book to Thomas Wotton, at whose estate Her Majesty would be visiting in her progress through Kent.

These letters rather obviously indicated Parker's method of casual but persistent recommendation of a person of interest to him, and the work of his protégé. Parker knew very well that Burghley might have forgotten the manuscript in the routine of his duties, so he took the occasion of the Queen's visiting Wotton in Boughton Malherbe, with the attendance of the Privy Council, as a means of recovering Lambarde's manuscript by associating it with Wotton on a particular date.

The Queen did go to Wotton's manor on August 17, 1573, and probably Lord Burghley had one of his clerks bring *A Perambulation of Kent* to Thomas Wotton. It might have been a conversation piece during some recreational period, as Parker, Burghley, and Wotton walked through the fragrance of the ripening apples along the lane through the orchard. Yet if these three influential persons discussed Lambarde's book on that occasion, there is no record of their conversation. On the other hand, Parker had brought Lambarde and his book to the attention of Burghley at an opportune time, when Wotton was the host and obviously much concerned with this manuscript. Surely no one could be with Wotton in Boughton Malherbe for very long without expressing his appreciation of the glorious Kentish scenery, and in the small change of relief from affairs of state, what better focal point could good talk have than a reference or two to the antiquity of this countryside, in particular to some forgotton relic that Lambarde had discovered and set down in his manuscript.

Yet if these great men had delayed publication of Lambarde's book as a result of their deliberations for three years, suddenly a new complication forced itself upon Lambarde. In the fall of 1573, his young wife died at the age of twenty, while apparently trying to give him the heir that he very much wanted. With this abrupt ending to his delight in her and the happy discovery of family life, Lambarde evidently lost all interest in his book. Whatever advice and approval had been forthcoming to him for his manuscript, he appeared to be in no mood to proceed with his writing.

Now the fine hand of Archbishop Parker appeared again as a guiding influence on Lambarde's life. Lambarde sought to assuage his grief by involving himself in new commitments that engaged his full attention. His decision to build a College for the Poor of Queen Elizabeth—which was probably Parker's suggestion—required much planning and a tremendous expenditure of money. In this instance, it was as if Lambarde were exhorted to follow the admonition of Jesus Christ to give half of his goods to the poor. Since this was to be the first Protestant hospital, there were no rules to follow and no examples to be imitated. First he had to obtain the necessary "pardons" from Her Majesty's government, in particular Lord Burghley's approval, in order to alienate the land for the building and the farms with which to endow this establishment.

The total expenditure, in amount of £2,642 5s. 6d., represented the cost of materials, labor, and the farms, the rent of which provided the endowment of the College. To say that this was the equivalent of one third of a million dollars has little significance. By any comparison with present scales of wages, the artisans, and even the artificers, received a pittance. Furthermore, land values in this particular area cannot now be appraised by any formula used in exchange of pounds for dollars because of the enormous increase in costs. That is to say, Lambarde's building and endowing of his College for the Poor was extremely generous at that time.

Some years later, a more satisfactory estimate of Lambarde's munificence did become available by comparison with another establishment similar to this one. When Lord Cobham died, he instructed the executors of his will to establish Cobham College on the principles used by Lambarde. He also designated Lambarde one of his executors, and Lambarde, in fact, became the president of Cobham College.

So the opportunity for close comparison between the two Colleges arose with only the allowance of twenty years intervening.

Lord Cobham was one of the richest men in the realm and had attained many high honors. He was a member of Elizabeth's Privy Council, Knight of the Garter, Lord Lieutenant of Kent, and Lord of the Cinque Ports, and at his death he was the Lord Chamberlain. The rents from his vast estates were reckoned by the manager for the heirs as more than £7,000 a year. His sons had received generous portions of the Cobham inheritance. When Cobham left £5,600 for the establishment of Cobham College, and an additional 2,000 marks in the value of furnishings for it, the rich Lord was giving away at his death not so much more than Lambarde's benefaction in middle age.[7] So if no one would minimize the generosity of Cobham's gift to the poor, Lambarde's magnanimity some twenty years earlier and without precedent, merits in the history of care of the poor more recognition than given it.

When Lambarde's great and considerate friend Archbishop Parker died at the age of seventy-one on May 17, 1575, two of Lambarde's important projects remained unfulfilled. *A Perambulation of Kent,* in which Parker had taken much interest and had sent to Lord Burghley, was still unprinted. And the College for the Poor of Queen Elizabeth had not yet been begun, although the acquisition of manors and farms for its endowment and the careful planning of the structure itself had passed the initial stages; in fact the actual building was not begun until August of that year. At this critical point in his career Lambarde needed Parker's advice and encouragement, for his humility and independence provided a second paradox, his diffidence and need of patronage to attain favor with Queen Elizabeth. Unlike many writers, Lambarde did not need money. However, Archbishop Parker had supplied the service of calling Lambarde's work to the attention of Lord Burghley and Queen Elizabeth.

Lambarde also needed Parker's leavening influence in the strident conflicts of religious faith. Although Parker had come under the influence of the teachings of Martin Luther while a student at Cambridge University, he was no fanatic. On the contrary, Lambarde seemed unwilling to yield his convictions to a liberal point of view. While Parker was a traditionalist intent upon preserving the Anglican Catholic Church, he was not an ardent reformer determined to have his own way rather than the middle course between Rome and reform. Lambarde was adamantly against Rome.

While the building of his College for the Poor was progressing, Lambarde apparently devoted much attention to the artisans and laborers as they performed their assigned tasks. He also recognized the need to establish rules of conduct for the persons who were to reside in this institution as well as some firm method for selecting these people. Such matters as these had long been established in the great Roman Catholic institutions for the care of the poor, but now almost forty years had passed since King Henry VIII's dissolution of the monasteries and other orders of the church. Moreover, Lambarde wished to make a distinction between the lazy and the sick. The recipients of his hospitality must be "poor, honest, and Godly persons who have been three years resident in the parish when they are chosen." [8] He wanted none of the vagabonds roaming the highways to be admitted. When he determined that accommodations could be provided for twenty persons, he also decided that the chief qualification must be their demonstrated piety. They were to be examined on the Creed, the Ten Commandments, and the Lord's Prayer, but in particular, he wished to be sure that they were anti-Popish.

The selection was to follow this formula: The two elder

wardens of the Drapers' Company would select one; another would be chosen by the steward of the manor of Greenwich from among the poor of the parish; the Drapers' Company of Greenwich would select one; the vicar and parish officers of Greenwich would select six; there would be one from Deptford, three from Lewisham, one from Tie, one from Altham, one from Charlton and Kidbrook, and one from Woolwich.

Lambarde himself composed a form of morning and evening prayer, with the consent of the Bishop of Rochester, and he ordained that these forms should always be used.[9] If, however, any of these prescriptions should become unlawful, by a change in the statutes of the realm, then the endowment of this College would become null and void. He directed that the control of his institution be given to the Master of the Rolls, the office that he himself held many years later, and that the handling of money for the maintenance derived from the endowment be conducted by the wardens of the Drapers' Company of London. As a symbol of their rule, he had a golden cup created, bearing the arms of Sir William Cordell, Master of the Rolls, and his own name engraved as the founder of the College for the Poor of Queen Elizabeth.[10] (This cup remained in the possession of the Drapers' Company of London long after the rest of the golden and silver plate belonging to that ancient guild had disappeared.)

Thus Lambarde determined the religious character of his establishment for all foreseeable time, even if the nation should return to Roman Catholicism as the state religion. He rather ingeniously arranged that in the leasing of the various farms for the endowment of his hospital, whenever the rents exceeded the requirements for maintenance, such money should accrue to his heirs, later revised to benefit his daughter. Lambarde had chosen these properties with such skill that after his death, the income increased so remarkably beyond the needs of the endowment that the wardens of the Drapers' Company recorded their embarrassment in providing substantial annuities to Lambarde's heirs; that is, the profits for the heirs exceeded the requirements of the benefactions. At the time of his gift, these properties represented a loss of income of £80 19s. 8d. a year, a substantial divestment of income from capital.

Yet much more important than either the expenditure of capital funds or the religious temper which he sought to maintain in the establishment was his recognition of the need for such institutions to care for the afflicted poor. Other men at this time gave their libraries, founded chairs in universities, and established foundations for various purposes, but the concept of providing a hospital for the poor of the local parishes began with Lambarde's benefactions. Various persons in the county were so impressed with the effectiveness of his organization that they left in their wills both large and small amounts to augment the endowment.[11] This was local approval of his institution and the way in which it was operated, and before long other men followed Lambarde's example in other counties. So, however local and parochial his contribution may appear after 350 years, a fair-minded appraisal of his College for the Poor would emphasize that it was a milestone in the history of the treatment of the poor.

The building was finished a year later in 1576. Lambarde's records of his disbursements indicate more than costs; actually the social structure of the community of artificers and artisans emerges from the tabulation of expenses.[12] These laborers worked a full day of twelve hours and more for a few pence a day, with which to buy food, lodging, and clothing. Hence, there was the need for just such a hospital as Lambarde was building and endowing for persons who had worked hard but had no substance accumulated when an accident disabled them.

His records of the farms that he purchased likewise indicate much more than the amount of his gift, for these emphasized the capital that had to be invested in order to receive approximately £81 per annum. One might assume that Lambarde expended approximately $60,000 in order to gain about $2400 per annum. Thus, the interest rate would be roughly 4 percent. These facts then hold interest for economic historians who observe that agriculture was not profitable, as well as for present-day American landowners, or persons with savings accounts. The increase in the value of land, however, later showed an important point about Lambarde's shrewdness; as already pointed out, the income increased beyond the requirements for endowment so that his heirs also received in later years annual disbursements from this endowment fund.

His pensioners soon discovered that they were not only provided with "house room" but also with "a private garden." There was also a "common garden" from which they would share the proceeds.[13] Moreover, each was given five shillings every month and two loads of wood. In these stipulations Lambarde was revealing a certain social philosophy of work in his thinking about the honest poor. Some years later, when the Kentish justices of the peace established the first House of Correction, this same concept of work and training appeared in the document Lambarde drew up for that novel institution, which soon became widely imitated. Up to then it had sufficed to send persons in difficulty with the law to jail (gaol) until jail delivery took place. During their incarceration, they received no training to assist them in working after they were released. Lambarde evidently believed that pensioners and prisoners alike should have the opportunity to work and to learn a trade of some kind while removed from society.

With the completion of his College, Lambarde apparently

recovered his composure through the multifarious duties that the building of the College had imposed upon his mind. At this time Thomas Wotton eventually began to draw Lambarde's attention back to *A Perambulation of Kent,* six years after Lambarde had first sent him the manuscript. Wotton seems to have then consented to write a Preface addressed to the men of Kent and offered to sponsor the printing of the book. And so Lambarde once more concentrated on the revision and correction of passages in his manuscript, in accord with the statements made in the Preface that he had since reworked the material. And so, after six years of delay, *A Perambulation of Kent* was printed in London in 1576.

This book greatly increased Lambarde's reputation, particularly in Kent, where now he was known as the benefactor of the College for the Poor and as a respected author of local history. If ever he had seemed an outsider, there was now no question of the esteem and affection in which he was held by the county families proud of their heritage. Yet the sale of the book was not so restricted as one might suppose; indeed, it was a part of the growing spirit of pride in being an Englishman to recall these ancient events that had transpired on English soil. Soon the poets and playwrights—Drayton, Greene, and Marlowe, and, of course, Shakespeare—were to appeal to the hearts and minds of Englishmen with stirring verses and chronicle plays about the illustrious past. Lambarde became known as the "Perambulator," and, incredible as it may seem in the light of what he actually accomplished, he is still referred to as the "Perambulator" by historians, as if his books on the law and his great efforts on behalf of the poor were secondary. The exemplary publication of the Kent Antiquarian Society, *Archaeologia Cantiana,* has had scarcely an issue through the many years of its being printed without an article or note referring to Lambarde's *A Perambulation of Kent.* These antiquarians have continued to refer to Lambarde's records as to an ultimate source book; and many persons have referred to *A Perambulation of Kent* for confirmation of their findings or as a stimulus for their research.

While Lambarde's name appears on various legal papers written during these years, he was evidently not establishing himself as a country lawyer. His avocation of antiquarian studies had apparently superseded his interest in his law profession. Probably the reception of *A Perambulation of Kent* encouraged him to continue with these studies, for it is known that at this time he had in mind giving similar treatment to all the other counties of England.

An unprinted manuscript of twenty-four pages, closely written, dealing with place names in various counties, has remained extant in the archives office in Maidstone, Kent.[14] Written in Latin, it has columns headed Anglo-Saxon, Welsh, and Latin, under which Lambarde has listed towns, villages, rivers, hills, and other places of interest, as if his intention were to classify these places under the languages used by the early settlers. By his use of languages, he thus was determining the ethnic groups and their customs. He also made a list of authorities, authors, and titles of books, as if he had in mind a much more elaborate treatise than this scholarly inquiry. Perhaps he had intended this paper as a sample of the book that he was projecting.

In 1730, 129 years after his death, there appeared an imposing volume entitled *Dictionarium Anglae Topographicum & Historicum,* which was represented as Lambarde's writing:

An Alphabetical Description of the Chief Places in England and Wales; With an Account of the most Memorable Events which have distinguish'd them. By the celebrated antiquary, formerly of Lincoln's-Inn, Esq.; and author of the Perambulation of Kent. Now first publish'd from a manuscript under the author's own hand. Printed for Fletcher Gyles, over-against Gray's Inn, Holborne. MDCCXXX.

Possibly this elaborate title page should be accepted, but surely these notes were not intended in their obviously unfinished form for publication. More likely than acceptance would be the compilation by another hand, probably the ambitious printer intent upon using Lambarde's material. *A Perambulation of Kent* had had at that time five editions, with a sixth to follow in 1826, and so it would seem probable that an industrious printer and bookseller intended to trade on Lambarde's reputation.

On the other hand, Lambarde had proposed to write this kind of book and was known to have progressed with it when he learned that William Camden was also writing a history of the antiquities of England, county by county. This book, which became Camden's celebrated *Britannia,* was well advanced at this time, although it was not printed until 1586. Camden was writing a narrative rather than an alphabetized series of notes, with a topographical and historical approach rather than a linguistic one. Each county formed a chapter in which he blended the historical events with the physical characteristics in a readable style. And so Lambarde made the decision to set aside his own book, possibly recognizing that his rather ingenious organization would not compensate for the fragmentation of his script into paragraphs arranged under the letters of the alphabet. Camden wrote the following heading for his chapter on Kent: "I am now come to Kent, a County, which William Lambard, a person eminent for learning and piety, describ'd so much to the life in that he left very little for those who come after him." Lambarde was evidently embarrassed by this high praise from the redoubtable Camden, and, upon seeing the manuscript, he admonished Camden to omit this heading.[15]

This abrupt ending of a project of study to which he might have devoted the next decade of his life forced Lambarde to reexamine his own ambitions for the future. At this point in his career, Lambarde appeared to have a haunting desire, however vaguely focused, to devote himself to the common good without remuneration commensurate with the hard work that would be necessary. The Commission of the Peace turned out to be precisely such an outlet for his energy. Whether the powerful hand of Lord Burghley reached out to tap him on the shoulder as appointee to the Commission of the Peace in Kent cannot be proved, but the great Treasurer's reading of *A Perambulation of Kent* would make such intercession probable. On the other hand, Thomas Wotton had sufficient influence with the Queen to bring about Lambarde's appointment, though this was scarcely an honor for a learned man. With this appointment, Lambarde was to demonstrate his tremendous energy and use his talents in standardizing the administration of English law at a time when England sorely needed a man with just these abilities.

At the meeting of the Council of Lincoln's Inn, held on February 9, 1579, William Lambarde was made an Associate of the Bench. The citation for this honor emphasized that he "hathe deserued universallie well of his comon welth and countrie, and likewyse of the Fellowshippe and Socyetie of this House." But in addition appeared a provision which was not to be taken as a precedent: "he shall have a roome to sytt amongest the Socyetie of the Felloweshippe of the Bench, as other Associats used to do, without enything payinge for the same." [16] This latter point implies special honor, since he had rooms and could afford the rent, despite having given nearly half of his fortune to the poor.

This honor, or recognition of Lambarde's learning, may

have coincided with his undertaking to examine the authentic records of the office of justice of the peace. It would be difficult to state on the basis of contradictory statements in the records precisely how long his inquiries had begun before his appointment to the Commission of the Peace. Indeed he might well have begun his examination of ancient rolls and books concerning this office without any consideration of such appointment, or he might well have been asked at an earlier date to accept appointment and then requested postponement. If such questions can be readily asked without evidence to provide the answer, then the point to be stressed would be that he entered the Commission of the Peace with this recognition from Lincoln's Inn. Although "Associate of the Bench" was not the highest honor to be conferred, it was a distinction not earned in the usual manner of barristers practicing the law. And Lambarde was to become a "Bencher" in good time.

Chapter 5

THE ACTIVE JUSTICE
(1580–1592)

Even before Lambarde took the oath of office, he assumed the responsibilities of being a justice of the peace with fervent energy. In April, 1580, according to Lambarde's "Ephemeris," or daybook, he accompanied Sir Christopher Alleyn, Sir Thomas Cobham, and Mr. Robert Byng in taking musters at five towns: Shorne, Friendsbury, Malling, Tunbridge, and Barowgreene.[1] This tedious duty of selecting men to defend the country against the rumored invasion by the Spaniards was time-consuming, and no doubt his assistance was welcomed by the overworked justices, but the reason he rushed into this problem characterized the man. While he was studying old and new statutes pertaining to the conduct of justices of the peace and examining old books and manuscripts dealing with this office, he was writing a book for his own use.

He had found work into which he could pour the life blood of his body as well as the distillation of his mind. He welcomed participation in the active work of the justice as a balance to his judgments formed by reading. And he had read with such discerning care that he had discovered discrepancies in the descriptions of the work of the justices as stated in the hastily revised Commission of the Peace. The phrasing of the Commission omitted several important duties indicated in the statutes. So when he wrote to Sir Thomas Bromley, the Lord Chancellor, to accept his appointment to the Commission, he asked him "to rectify" these errors and "some other crookedness," which he had found during the preparation of a manual to guide him in his work as a justice.

This audacious letter from a tyro on the Commission to the chief of Elizabeth's government again indicated Lambarde's lack of tact. As a scholar, he was annoyed with inaccuracy, but he was incapable of using a graceful approach to the situation, which must have proved very embarrassing to the newly appointed Chancellor. Although in this letter Lambarde highly praised Bromley's superior knowledge of the law, he set himself up as the authority.

Bromley did absolutely nothing about changing the wording of the Commission; nor did he do anything for Lambarde. Bromley was a career man, who had attended Oxford University and the Inner Temple. Upon the death of Sir Nicholas Bacon, Lord Keeper of the Great Seal, who is chiefly remembered today as the father of the more famous Sir Francis Bacon, Queen Elizabeth was forced to choose a successor to this high office. Bacon's executive powers had probably been second only to Burghley's, but he had allowed the work of the justices of the peace to decline in effectiveness because he had failed to eliminate from the rolls those who were incompetent and indolent. For there were indeed many country squires who liked being justices of the peace but neglected to work in this important office.

Sir Thomas Bromley had risen to power chiefly because of the Earl of Leicester; yet both Lord Burghley and Her Majesty's uncle Lord Hunsdon had regarded him with approbation; they too had extended favors to him. Elizabeth needed a man in this high office acceptable to both factions in her divided Privy Council. Although he was not skilled in the law, a lawyer's lawyer, he had proved his loyalty to his Queen in the trial of the Duke of Norfolk for high treason and had urged Mary Queen of Scots to renounce her claim to the throne of England. He had exhibited such charm and skill in playing both factions of the Privy Council against one another that he seemed to the Queen more likely to succeed as Lord Chancellor than would Attorney General Gerrand, who had thorough knowledge of the law; besides, Bromley was her favorite dancing partner.[2]

As soon as she had chosen Bromley, she instructed him to revise the articles of the Commission of the Peace and extend the power of these justices. She also instructed him to dismiss certain incompetent persons and make new appointments. Both of these tasks required knowledge that he evidently did not have. He did not understand the problems of local government or the functioning of the justices of the peace, and he was not acquainted with persons appropriate for appointment, although he did appoint William Lambarde. Somehow he muddled through the revision of the Commission, making errors and leaving omissions about which no one apparently cared except Lambarde.

Since there were hundreds of justices of peace in the realm, Bromley had to depend upon recommendations. Each county had its group; at this time, there were eighty-eight in Kent, thirteen in Rutland, forty-seven in Sussex, and forty-six in Suffolk.

If a justice was dedicated, the demands on him were severe, but in any case, the remuneration of two shillings a day, as Lambarde later observed, scarcely paid for travel expenses. The justices of the peace assembled four times each year at their quarter sessions in the county town, Maidstone in Kent: Michaelmas Term (October), Hilary or Epiphany (January), Easter (early spring), and the Translation of St.

Thomas (midsummer). The midsummer and autumn sessions came during the harvest seasons when work was heavy on the farms; the winter session usually was in the midst of inclement weather when the roads were impassable. Hence the session after Easter had become the most important assembly in the year. Then wages were fixed and the assignments made to repair bridges and roads, to make accountings for the poor, as well as to hear and determine cases "bound over" by the justices acting singly or in pairs during the period between sessions.

The record of how Lambarde became interested in and involved with the study of the jurisdiction of the justice of the peace has become confused by his own statements. Although there is no doubt whatsoever that he did an enormous amount of work on this subject, his letter to the Lord Chancellor at the time of his appointment has given the impression that he began the work which led to the printing of *Eirenarcha* in the interim between his appointment and his acceptance of it.[3] So much learning supports this book, however, that it seems absurd to assume that he had not already undertaken this study even if *Eirenarcha* itself did not become his purpose until later. According to the record in his "Ephemeris," which he kept from 1580 to 1588, he plunged headlong into his duties before he was officially installed. He then recognized, he wrote, that he needed some guide to this practice and began reading earlier books and manuals on this subject. In this manner he composed his *Eirenarcha*, as the title in anglicized Greek indicates, the office of the justice of the peace. This book included both the history of the office and the practical application of these duties in practice. Although there can be no doubt that Lambarde's interest in the practical procedures for carrying out the justice of the peace's responsibilities came with his appointment, it seems equally obvious that the writing of the history of this office required more time than the few months of concentrated effort otherwise permitted for this task.[4]

His thinking rested on the premise that the laws of England were good, and the dreadfully severe punishments necessary. He was not a reformer of the law but a standardizer of the administration of the law. The system was adequate but the application casual and even careless. Here was work to be done.

It was customary for justices of the peace to work in pairs outside the quarter sessions, and frequently Lambarde heard and determined cases with his father-in-law, George Multon. During June and July, 1580, he examined with Multon several persons involved in robbery. The complaint against them had not come from the local people but from a writ executed by the Privy Council. So after these examinations, he sent his findings to the "Lord Chief Baron." There were several cases of this type during his first summer in office. On at least one of them, he wrote the findings that he and Multon had made to Sir Thomas Walsingham.

On August 26, he rode to Tunbridge to serve on a Commission of Sewers for Medway, and while there he assisted Sir Thomas Fane and Sir Christopher Alleyn in sentencing an alehouse keeper to jail for not observing a previous order by the justices to close up shop. On September 20, with Multon, he sent another alehouse keeper to jail. And on the basis of a writ from the Privy Council they took testimony from a man whom they bound over to the quarter sessions. In another case at Ightham they took "sureties" for a man to appear at the quarter sessions, and later released the tailor and shoemaker who had provided the sureties. The distinction between sureties and bailment Lambarde explained with some care later in his manual for justices. (The justices here bound over certain persons, together with the alleged offender, to appear as witnesses at the quarter sessions and attempted to secure their appearance with sums of money; whereas in bailment, goods or money would be posted to secure the appearance of the alleged offender.)

On September 26, Lambarde with Sir Thomas Fane took sureties that an alehouse keeper would close his business; then on the next two days with Lord Cobham, Lambarde assisted in licensing several keepers of alehouses in their dwellings. Despite his duties as Lord Lieutenant of the Shire, Cobham took an active part in the Commission of the Peace, being director of the Western Division, which included the lathe of Aylesford, to which Lambarde was assigned. Cobham was also Lord of the Cinque Ports, and consequently involved in meeting and entertaining envoys and distinguished visitors from the Continent on their way to Elizabeth's court. Yet he personally was licensing keepers of alehouses. Sir Thomas Fane's name also appeared several times in Lambarde's "Ephemeris" this first year. So Lambarde was associated on the one hand with very distinguished persons while, on the other hand, he was dealing with people who could not keep out of trouble.

To the bishop he certified, with Multon, the good behavior of a girl about to be married, a further extension of the duties of these justices. Then with Multon he bound over several persons to the quarter sessions held on October 4, at which time he certified various cases which he had heard and determined, as well as several recognizances.

Late in the month he reported to the Lord Chief Baron his examination of a person who maintained an unlicensed alehouse. In November, acting with Multon, he ordered the shipping of two men and two women involved in cases of bastardy, and accepted payments in order to relieve the parish of the expense of maintaining the bastards. Four days later, again with Multon, he ordered the scourging of a woman for bearing a bastard; and that night he wrote a letter to Sir Thomas Walsingham about Reignold Peckham, who had used the name of Thomas Clark. This incident supplied an insight to one of the ways in which Walsingham learned of traitors and spys in the realm, for the next day Walsingham directed Lambarde to send Peckham to the Lord Chief Baron in London.

Even the celebration of Christmas was interrupted by having to send a man to jail for stealing nineteen sheep. Multon and Lambarde then accepted £20 from another person in recognizance to give evidence at the next jail delivery.

Meanwhile Lambarde's work on his manual for justices had developed to the point where he would print it. So during the first months of 1581 he appeared only a few times with Multon to hear and determine routine cases. He did, however, go to Tunbridge to act with Sir Thomas Fane on a curious case of a renegade physician; he did certify cases at the quarter sessions that spring; and the following day, with Multon, he took "obligations" from a man and woman for the keep of their bastard. Since a "general pardon" was expected, they did not proceed to order punishment; furthermore, the support of the child was arranged.

At this time Lambarde's handbook for justices, *Eirenarcha*, came from a London printing press, and the first printing was sold out.[5] The year was 1581; the book contained more than six hundred pages divided into two parts: first, a history of the justices of the peace, and second, the procedures for justices to follow in acting alone or with another justice, and how to conduct the quarter sessions. This first edition is not usually mentioned by historians, who have seemed to prefer the later expanded editions. The first edition is, however, very interesting and provides insights into the situation of the justices of the peace in 1581 when their authority was extended. But Lambarde audaciously used his letter to Lord Chancellor Bromley as the preface to *Eirenarcha*, to indicate just how inaccurately stated was this intended extension of authority.

His purpose in writing Book I extended beyond a simple history of this office; he obviously thought it necessary at this time to inspire respect for the office and establish pride in being a part of this ancient service to king and country, as he digressed from the description of the development of the justices to deal with the vexatious problem of why the visiting justices came from the King's Bench in Westminister twice a year to conduct the Assizes throughout the counties. He pointed out that when the King's Court was instituted, there was simultaneous recognition that the judges of the King's Court must travel to the counties to hear and determine local cases; and so the Court of Assize was of equal antiquity to the King's Court.

He cited the statute enacted in 1350 to organize the conservators of the peace and another statute ten years later to permit these keepers of the peace to arrest offenders and to hear and determine cases of felony and trespass under the authority of the Chief Justicer, an officer whose authority evidently aroused Lambarde's curiosity. He further digressed to explain that the Chief Justicer had authority to govern in the King's absence. In other words, Lambarde was establishing the authority of present justices of the peace as answerable only to the Crown, or the Privy Council, as their ancient counterparts reported to the Chief Justicer. In this way he endeavored to distinguish between the overlapping jurisdictions of the judges of Assize and the justices of the peace in their quarter sessions.

In Book II he sought to make more practicable the various procedures of the justices alone, acting together, and in conducting the quarter sessions; he gave illustrations using the names of living justices in Kent—Multon, Fane, and others he knew intimately—in the various forms of legal writs, orders, and reports. This common touch made his illustrations practical rather than theoretical; it also implied that these men were already using the book, as indeed the book was familiar to them in manuscript form. The use of these names certainly enlivened the illustrations, and this device amounted to genius.

In this first edition he explained that he had asked Mr. John Tyndall, "a friend and fellow of mine in Lincoln's Inn," to cull out all the statutes with which the justices had to deal and to arrange them for ready reference. Although Lambarde had used these statutes to give authority to the procedures he was recommending, he evidently recognized that many readers of his book were unfamiliar with the statutes and in particular with the new ones. He apparently envisioned a well-informed gentry on the bench of the quarter sessions. But to make such recommendations indicated that he understood the total inadequacy of many of his associates. And the Queen's frequent concern with appointments to the Commission and the elimination of incompetent persons from the lists of justices would fully support Lambarde's view.

As some years later Dorothy Osborne, a seventeenth-century country woman, wrote to her prospective husband with some scorn about these country gentlemen whose aim was no higher than to be justice of the peace or High Sheriff for a term, all of Lambarde's struggles to educate these squires, devoted to their hawks and dogs, would seem to have been in vain.[6] The justices had fallen into such disrepute that Shakespeare could satirize them in the persons of Shallow and Silence in his plays. And without Lambarde's *Eirenarcha* conditions in these local courts could have reached the nadir of justice.

There were several handbooks for justices before Lam-

barde ever conceived of writing his—notably, Fitzherbert's
Justice of the Peace ⁷—but these were old and out of print
and lacked all the recent statutes over which the justices were
now given the execution. Queen Elizabeth's interest in local
government led her to instruct her new Lord Chancellor to
curtail the duties of the High Sheriff and increase those of
the Lord Lieutenants in the various counties. As a result, the
High Sheriff's position became more honorary as an Officer
of the Crown to raise money, whereas the Lord Lieutenant
assumed the responsibility of working with the justices. The
judges of Assize remained examiners of the determinations
made by the justices and arbiters in certain difficult criminal
cases, as well as totally in charge of all civil cases.

In preparing *Eirenarcha* Lambarde had examined Mar-
row's *Readings* and Fitzherbert's traditional handbook for
justices. But on finding these works no longer adequate, he
began to read "old and new books" of the common law, volumes of acts and statutes, until he made, as he wrote the
Chancellor, "a module" of his own book. His desire to supply
the gentry who were "not trained up" in the study of the
law might have only historical significance today, but this
book revealed much about the treatment of vagabonds,
rogues, Gypsies (called Egyptians), palmists, fencers, bear-
wardens, players of interludes, and minstrels unattached to
some great lord. In addition, there were itinerate tinkers and
peddlers on the roads for whom the justices had to order
whippings or boring of ears, if they returned within sixty
days or lacked licenses from a justice. In each instance, Lambarde provided the penalty that the justice should use, as
well as the form to copy for the court order.

These justices were charged in a statute in 1563, with the
care and relief of the poor. Collections of funds were com-
pulsory and augmented by money deposited in the poor
boxes of the church. But the parish priests or preachers often

shared the same parish offices with the justices in administering relief to the poor. As a result of this divided responsibility, the system had varied effectiveness. Consequently in the decade preceding *Eirenarcha*, Parliament began enacting a series of laws for relief of the poor.

Such were the conditions that made *Eirenarcha* indispensable. If for no other reason than the proper treatment of the parish poor, in contrast to the strangers on the highways, the justices found Lambarde's handbook useful; yet of course this was only one major problem confronting these private men in their public service. They required examples to copy in writing court orders not only for the local officers to execute but also for their reports of the hearings and determinations to the appropriate lord in the Privy Council. The keeper of these records, the *Custos Rotulorum* was one of the *Quorum*, or group competent to write such orders.

At the quarter sessions on March 22, 1581, Lambarde certified the cases of those persons that he had bound over to this session. He had evidently prepared a Charge to the Jurors, but he did not use it; indeed, he might have misdated this manuscript for it was applicable to a case of riot occurring on Tuesday, May 13; so the inference drawn is that he confused March and May in his later endorsement of this Charge and took the date of the quarter sessions rather than the date of the special hearing that he held for the case of riot. An extant court order made certain the date of the Charge to the Jurors in May, not March.

Evidently about twenty rioters, some on horse and others on foot, congregated to destroy a house inhabited by a couple. The cause is unclear, but a new law prescribed a certain acreage around new dwellings. Yet the apparent animosity in this attack would suggest the possibility of religious persecution rather than lack of four acres around the house. The attempt to cut down the foundations failed, the house was set on fire. The house was located in a lonely place in Longroleshoth and occupied by William Stratford and his wife. It had been built and was owned by Thomas Culpepper. And since the Culpeppers, Darrels, Guildfords, and Finches were among the Kentish families that remained most obstinately recusant, the question would arise whether the attack was directed more at Culpepper than at the Stratfords who suffered this outrageous attack.

Lambarde lost his judicial calm in discussing this incident with the jurors. It would be to his credit if the issue involved the Roman Catholics, as he was aroused to see that justice prevailed. The human right of this couple to be protected from unjust attack, he pointed out, was more important than the loss of property that they had thus sustained. In all of his reading of history and ancient law he had found nothing comparable to the bestial action of these "night riders." He reminded the jurors that King Canute had laws against breaking into houses, and the penalty for so doing was death. Now in this instance, Lambarde shouted, the law craved a double death.

There was good reason for him to emphasize the severest penalty, for some of the twenty or more men came from among the neighbors and friends here assembled, "our own countrymen and neighbors." Hence, though Lambarde could expect little cooperation from the jurors, he intended to frighten the wits out of them with threats of punishments in order to get the necessary identification of even a few of the rioters. He warned that these "night riders" might proceed to "some other thing," if left unpunished, and would prove to be "infamous for this our shire with all posterity." He used both fear and shame to wring out some guide to the culprits. As he made no entry of this "frightful affray" in his "Ephemeris," he was not certifying this case to the quarter sessions but directly to the Court of Star Chamber.

These extracts from Lambarde's "Ephemeris" from 1580 to 1588 indicate the kind of petty and violent criminal cases which Lambarde, the historian of the law, was called upon to hear and determine. Moreover these extracts indicate the cross-currents of ordinary life among the people, not in the highly congested areas of London's low life but in the country, in a county favored for climate and agricultural opportunities. The condition that Kent provided the highway to the Cinque Ports, the gateways to travel in Europe, made possible a variety of problems arising from vagabonds, wanderers, and the infiltration of seminarians and foreign spies.

Lambarde's daily life, however, was not entirely devoted to his ardent participation in the Commission of the Peace. He was a lawyer whose services evidently were in demand among his neighbors and friends, transferring titles to lands, settling estates, and performing various legal services. He was also a country squire interested in buying and selling manors and farms for his own profit. But in term time he evidently spent much time in London, journeying between Westcombe or St. Cleres to Lincoln's Inn, where he maintained his rooms throughout his life.

It is idle speculation, perhaps, to inquire how much time he spent with his brother, Giles, who encountered one problem after another in the drapery business. He appears, however, to have become well acquainted with his brother's wife and to have formed a very high opinion of her. In later years he twice showed his esteem for her, and since his standards were extremely high, Margery must have been an exemplary person. Yet she had no children from her marriage with Giles Lambarde, and an heir was an important criterion of a successful marriage. Whoever were Lambarde's friends outside the precincts of Lincoln's Inn has remained unknown, as is the case with his mother's family, the Hornes, and in particular his mother's sister, Mistress Bond. The so-called

Lambarde *Diary* records only facts, births, baptisms, marriages, children, and deaths, none of the tremendous trifles
that reveal character, which one finds in the *Diary* of Samuel
Pepys.

On May 30, 1581, Lambarde's brother, Giles, died in London at the age of forty-three. He made no mention of William
in his will. His chief concern seemed to be the relief of his
cousin Thomas Wicken, who was bound with him in a large
debt to William Elkin. Evidently Giles was not successful
as a draper. Indeed, he had had trouble with tenants from
the time he received his inheritance from the Court of
Wards. Now he had named his wife Margery and Thomas
Wicken as his executors. The property left to Margery corresponded to the mansions, tenements, and messuages listed
in his father's will. Giles gave an annuity to his mother's
brother, John Horne, and remembered well his cousin, the
son of his mother's sister, who had seven children for whose
future Giles seemed concerned. Possibly some estrangement
between William and Giles might at some time have developed.

During the summer months in Kent there were several
brawls and street fights requiring the attention of Lambarde
and other justices. Some of these offenders were bound over
to the next quarter sessions while others gave sureties to
maintain the peace. These sureties usually amounted to £5,
but one was as much as £20. These brawls indicated the general restiveness among persons able to pay rather high fines
for disturbing the peace.

Repairs to the Hockenbury Bridge required an assessment
be paid of £12 15s., agreed upon by the justices in Lord
Cobham's division. Here was an example of how local repairs
were provided by levies on the persons holding property in
the area that followed the course of the Medway River. The
justices determined the amount, proceeded to collect it, and

then hired the laborers to do the work; all these activities required much time as well as the expenditure of their own money.

With Multon and Sir Christopher Alleyn, Lambarde examined eight rogues, dressed in the apparel of "Egyptians," and sent them to jail. But for the remainder of the year 1581, Lambarde's cases were merely routine, taking of sureties and binding culprits over to the next quarter sessions. However these required his time and energy, even though they were routine, and he apparently continued to ride around the Lathe of Aylesford to hear and determine uninteresting felonies and misdemeanors as if he personally had responsibility beyond the endeavors of his fellows. In middle age he appeared more like a younger man, eager to gain all the experience available. The large number of other justices with whom he worked indicated that he was not content to stay at home with George Multon and take care of the problems around Ightham; he traveled throughout the division headed by Lord Cobham and beyond that district. Perhaps it was pride that motivated this apparent compulsion to be useful. Probably he was trying to learn about every contingency of the life of a justice as he prepared to revise *Eirenarcha*.

In January, 1582, the printers of *Eirenarcha* were involved in a legal contest over the printing of the second issue of this valuable handbook. R. Tottle and C. Barker, who had printed the octavo volume in 1581, wished to reissue it, and they found that R. Newbury and H. Bynneman wanted to print 1,500 copies for their own sale. In contrast to poets and playwrights at this time, who needed to have patrons pay for the expense of printing their books, Lambarde had a book for which there was sufficient demand and consequent profit to the printers that they could have a lawsuit over it. Legal items in the printers' lists were indeed valuable because there were men with sufficient means to buy books useful to them in their profession of the law.

Lambarde meanwhile was hearing and determining all manner of cases, one of which illustrated how a local officer could assume duties of another. A borsholder in Milton arrested a culprit, fined him, or took sureties, as the phrase is "told the money"—that is to say, he counted the money. The arrest ordinarily would have been made by the constable; in this instance the constable was absent; the borsholder found the culprit stealing. Lambarde reviewed the procedure and certified this case along with others at the quarter sessions on April 24.

At that quarter sessions he delivered the Charge to the Jurors in an interesting pattern that he had developed for this purpose. He spoke of the offenses as if they were committed against God, and only secondarily against the law over which the sovereign presided as God's deputy. He reminded the jurors, furthermore, that their oaths were not to be taken lightly as if they were repeating prayers with their lips while their minds were on other subjects. He asked what would happen if the laws were not enforced by severe penalties. He tried to explain the process of the law from the Queen as the "supreme executioner of all her laws," through her justices to the jurors sworn to inquire of offenders.

He did not stress the difficulty with the system; namely, that the sheriff recruited these jurors from the shopkeepers and yeomen, the citizens who had little to gain from reporting on their neighbors and friends who became involved in unlawful games, begetting bastards, and in the various forms of trying unlawfully to gain higher prices for their grains. As any reader of Sir Thomas Smith's *De republica Anglorum* (1583) would know, England was monarchial and aristocratic; many of the low class had no vote. These for the most part were the workers and idlers who got into trouble.

Lambarde mixed his metaphors somewhat in trying to illustrate his explanations. First he spoke of the Queen as the physician healing the sores of the commonwealth; then she was the gardener weeding out the overgrown stalks and trimming the branches of sour fruit. Finally, he pointed out that the jurors seemed to expect the complaints to be ready in this place rather than to inquire diligently and present evildoers from their own experience.

One curious eccentricity that Lambarde manifested was his habit of signing these Charges with his name written in Anglo-Saxon characters. Yet in so doing, he evidently had in mind that these Charges which he had preserved would someday be of interest; he would then remind his readers of his Anglo-Saxon learning. He was right in both instances. But although legal historians have carefully examined both his books and those written by other writers of his time, they long overlooked these Charges to the Jurors as of no consequence. Yet these Charges reveal how a learned man tried very hard to explain to illiterate auditors, or at least to persons unfamiliar with the technicalities of the law, precisely what the system and the philosophy undergirding it were. Surely a man who sought to improve the minds of the jurors and to make them grasp what they basically were doing beyond serving out their duties had great patience and a tremendous desire to bring the theory of justice to the common people. That was his democratic vision, a vision cherished while others with learning and authority laughed at these people's stupidity and evidently failed to grasp what Lambarde was attempting almost alone to accomplish for the common good. He reemphasized the spirit of cooperation and thus sought to make the people recognize that they were a part of the legal system and, as he repeated, held the enforcement of law in their own hands.

On May 16, 1582, Stephen Vallenger was given summary trial in the Star Chamber on the circumstantial evidence that Roman Catholic pamphlets were found in his lodging. Antwerp was usually the place of publication given on the title page of such pamphlets, although many were printed in England in this manner. The significance was that the fear of invasion, or of an uprising of the recusant Roman Catholics, had quite taken away the reasoning of the Privy Council. The court order finding Vallenger guilty has remained through the years: his ears were cut off; he paid a severe fine; he was put in the pillory; and he was finally sentenced to ten years in prison.[8]

Perhaps Vallenger was known and watched as a Papist. But the nominal Protestantism of Elizabeth and her peers would scarcely explain such an example being made of an alleged Roman Catholic, at a time when rich men of like persuasion remained unmolested. It was an example set before the common people of how a comman man could be punished for his faith. And though Lambarde was against the Roman Catholics per se, he stood boldly for equal justice for rich and poor.

The severe penalties meted out to Stephen Vallenger apparently weighed heavily on Lambarde's mind; at least he investigated the early statutes, going back to the time of King Edward III, "who made the first law that I find against them (rogues)," and continued his search for precedents to the time of "our good Queen." He enumerated these penalties—cutting away of ears, branding with a letter, and death for vagabonds, beggars, and loiterers—when, within a month of the Star Chamber proceedings, on June 14, 1582, a special sessions to inquire of rogues convened at Maidstone. Although he emphasized the uncleanliness, lewd talk, and pilfering of these wayfarers, he evidently was well aware that there were many recusants in Kent and so he avoided in this Charge to the Jurors stating that the danger actually consisted of seminarians and foreigners of the Roman Catholic faith. But he quoted the Bible that man must live by the sweat of his brow in order to eat. So it was the jurors' duty to God and to Her Majesty to seek out these rogues and set an example against such evildoing at home.

Routine binding over of culprits occupied much of Lambarde's attention for the remainder of the year. On December 5, however, a case occurred that indicated an enormous waste of judicial talent on the hearing and determining of a felony, the taking of a piece of cloth. Here were Lord Cobham, Sir Christopher Alleyn, and Lambarde arrayed in judicial splendor for a stupid lout who had stolen a piece of cloth.

Another case reveals how Lambarde's sense of humor occasionally filtered through his serious manner, though possibly in this instance it happened quite unconsciously. With his father-in-law, he took orders for the support of a bastard, whose mother was Susan Waters and father was Richard Cowper, "as we thought." The bond was six pence a week. That a baby could be supplied with necessities for six pence a week indicates the purchasing power of a penny at that time, but even this provision was curious, since apparently the mother could afford that amount. Probably Susan Waters was so promiscuous that Lambarde's phrase about the probable father, "as we thought," was actually appropriate rather than whimsical.

The year 1583 began the period that Lambarde described in various letters as "my halcyon days," but it began ordinarily enough. Someone had charged Sir Christopher Alleyn with recusancy, but apparently the charge was dropped, for Sir Christopher continued to appear with Lambarde at numerous hearings. Lambarde wrote himself a reminder in his "Ephemeris" to remit at the Easter quarter session his Register of the Poor at Ightham. Presumably George Multon, now in his eighties, had usually made this listing, and might have been ill at that time. This item would indicate, however, that Lambarde was still staying with Multon at St. Cleres, Ightham, and consequently had taken time for this additional duty. His interest in the relief of the poor, furthermore, would prompt him to discover the facts at first hand.

The routine cases of 1583, spelled out in Lambarde's "Ephemeris," need not be reviewed here, although a double murder case involving Thomas Heywood and a woman named Parnel, whom he married, titulates the imagination. Parnel's former husband, William Brightrede, was found murdered, as was Thomas Heywood's wife. Since these murders were evidently committed before the marriage of Heywood and Parnel, the details must have indeed been fascinating, but apparently not to Lambarde; his record ends with sending Heywood and Parnel to jail.

During this period Lambarde was associated with Sir Christopher Alleyn, George Multon, Fane, Twysden, and Richters, and John Lennard, an indication of how active Lambarde was as a justice of the peace. It seems that Lambarde moved from one village or town to another and conducted the hearings and determinations in association with the person residing in the particular place.

The Kent justices were far in advance of others in their decision to build a House of Correction. Lambarde had attended the Assizes at Rochester on that day, March 4, 1583, at which he certified recognizances; then the justices assembled and presented to the judges of Assize their plan for caring for the poor who were neither sick nor in any way afflicted, but yet refused to work. Lambarde wrote the draft of this proposal, and presumably it had to be submitted to the visiting judges of the Assizes. This was a momentous development insomuch as these local justices were thus attempting to make practicable one of the new laws Parliament was providing for the relief of the poor. Heretofore beating of idlers seemed to be the only remedy for the lazy; sometimes the justices sent these idlers to jail, but the jails were overcrowded with felons. So at last these Kentish justices had advanced a plan for attempting to rehabilitate certain persons in the local parishes in this newly conceived House of Correction.

Probably this idea originated with Lambarde, since he had built with his own money a College for the deserving, or afflicted, poor. This House of Correction provided relief for another group in the county; namely, those who were healthy but lazy.

On this same momentous day the justices wrote a defense of a local constable who had been arrested by a "Knight Marshal's man," on the complaint of a purveyor. This purveyor, a petty officer of the royal household, had come into Kent and set a price on certain commodities and then met resistance from the local constable; whereupon, on the complaint of this purveyor, the Knight Marshal had sent his deputy to arrest the constable. But the justices had courage enough to defend their local officer against the charge. Here again might be Lambarde's sturdy defiance of persons in high places who sought to take advantage of a poor man. Lambarde was fighting for equal justice and evidently he had persuaded his fellow justices to permit him to write this letter. He alone among the various justices whose careers were recorded seemed to care not at all what some superior person might think of him.

Lambarde recognized, furthermore, that the weakest link in the chain of local justice was the constable. These officers served without any remuneration and were appointed to their duties by a justice of the peace. Yet, as Lambarde realized, many of these constables could not read or write; the justices issued court orders to them as if they were able to read the name of the culprit to be arrested and confined in the jail. Often enough a shrewd culprit assisted the constable in reading the order and, upon finding his own name, absented himself from the community before some other person pointed out his identity to the constable. Shakespeare's portrayals of Dogberry and Vergus were satiric, but not so exaggerated for comedy that they did not apply to real life.

To remedy the confusion about the various duties to which parish officers were assigned, and, in particular, to define the duties of the constable and to improve standards, Lambarde was preparing a handbook entitled *The Duties of Constables, Borsholders, Tythingmen, and such other lowe Ministers of the Peace.* This, like *Eirenarcha,* was another practical book that required not only knowledge of the development of these various parish offices but also experience in recognizing abuses of the persons assigned to these duties. This book appeared in print in 1583 and like *Eirenarcha* supplied much-needed information. Hence it too had a remarkable sale of the first edition.

Lambarde was preparing a second edition of *Eirenarcha,* though two subsequent issues of the first edition were supplying the demand; he wanted to elaborate upon the directions given to the justices and to expand the second part of his book into three parts. New statutes were now coming from the Parliament for the justices to administer; ordinances for special duties were issued by the Crown and the Privy Council. The bewildered justices were falling far behind in their understanding of their additional duties, and it was incumbent upon Lambarde to bring their knowledge up to the present situation.

In the midst of all these activities, Lambarde moved to Halling on May 15, 1583. He was intent upon wooing a widow who lived in the historic bishop's palace of Halling. Her name was Sylvestria Dean Dalison, and she was born in 1554, the year after her father, Robert Dean, had acquired Halling Palace by means of a ninety-nine year lease from John Scory, the Bishop of Rochester. Robert Dean had married the daughter of Richard Woodward, and Sylvestria was their sole heir. Her marriage to William Dalison, the son of the justice by that name, had taken place in 1573, and they had had two children, a son named Maximilian and a daughter, Sylvestria. Her first husband had been dead for two years when Lambarde came to Halling. She was a warm and lovable person, devoted to her children and very lonely, at twenty-nine, in her large and beautifully situated palace, overlooking the Medway River and a short canter from Cobham Hall, where "my father-like good Lord" resided. There was every reason for Lambarde to fall in love with Sylvestria.

Meanwhile Parliament had enacted a stringent statute concerning rogues, and on May 21, 1583, Lambarde attended a special assembly to deal with rogues who were forthwith by his order bound and whipped. On this occasion he delivered the Charge to the Jurors and recommended severe penalties. He pointed out that the laws of the realm were grounded upon the laws of God and nature itself. He cited scripture against idleness: "In the sweate of thy browes shalt thou eate this breade." And he quoted from St. Paul: "Whosoever will not laboure, shall not eate." These old spellings as well as the phrasing suggested that he might be using the Geneva Bible. Possibly, however, since there was Gundulph's Latin Bible in the library of the Priory of St. Andrew, Rochester, Lambarde, with his love of Latin, might have translated from the Latin Bible generally known as St.

Jerome's. This Charge repeated many ideas used on June 14, 1582.

The severe beating of wayfarers and idle persons did not deter Lambarde from recognizing the necessity of beggars. For on this same day of ordering a rather large number of rogues to be whipped, he gave a license to Thomas Godfrey, whose house had burned, to beg until Allhallowstide within the limits of Lord Cobham's vast estate. In these times, when a poor man lost his home in a fire, all he could do was beg along the highway, and thus gain a pittance of relief as he carried his license from door to door, or implored assistance of passersby. The restoration of his burned house could scarcely be expected.

Lambarde bound over on June 23 a yeoman and clothier to appear at the next quarter sessions "by force of a supplication out of Chancery." Evidently one or the other had successfully petitioned the "long arm of the queen's mercy," vested in the Chancery, for a hearing of this dispute. As neither was a person of importance, this action illustrated the way in which a lowly person could find relief extended from the highest court to the local community.

Review for relief of the poor was established by the justices, as when on July 13 Lord Cobham and Lambarde decided that the rate should be eleven pence on the pound of land evaluation. This amount was to be raised before Allhallows Day.

Two days later Lambarde certified recognizances and examinations that he had made to the Assizes in Maidstone, and three days later by direction of Sir Thomas Gawdy, one of the judges of Assize, he wrote to the Vicar of Sevenoaks. Two days later Lambarde again wrote directions, this time in association with Lord Cobham and Sir Christopher Alleyn, for the constables to collect the money required for both the keeping of the jail and the recently established House of Correction.

The increasing number of instances in which Lambarde wrote the court orders of various kinds indicates that he was continuing as one of the *Quorum* and also the *Custos Rotulorum*. Few of the justices had the knowledge of such forms as Lambarde had, and those who had the skill were reluctant to spend many hours at such work. But now that Lambarde had moved to Halling, he was being used much more by Lord Cobham.

In association with Lord Cobham, Lambarde heard and determined three cases, on August 20, that represented a large number of problems confronting the justices of the peace. First was bastardy, involving punishment and sustenance for the child. If the father could not be identified, then the parish had to find the means. In this instance Marie Rice was able to accuse a man named Hall; the pair had to pay eight pence per week for the care of the child, although marriage was evidently not a consideration. Except for contributing to the keep of the child, the father remained unpunished, but the mother, as was the usual custom, had to appear in the public square stripped to the waist and receive on her bare back a certain number of lashes. The theory was to make an example of the poor wench so that other girls in the parish would be frightened. However, judging from the frequent cases of bastardy, copulation and conception continued unabated. A second case concerned a woman named Marie Grafton, who, having refused to serve in accordance with her covenant, was sent to the House of Correction. This is an example of the humane treatment accorded to the poor who had no defense against the accusations of their employers. Another labor problem was that of James Butler in the Parish of Meopham, who had "given honest labor" but whom, nevertheless, the parish officers wished to expel.

Lambarde ordered that Butler remain in Meopham since he had worked there for four years.

At the quarter sessions in Maidstone, on September 24, 1583, Lambarde certified various recognizances, including one for an alehouse keeper; he also gave the Charge to the Jurors. This was one of his finest explanations of his own theory of justice. After beginning with his customary reminder that the jurors were to discover evildoers in order that the justices could determine the penalties, he elaborated upon his usual formula that their service was for the glory of God and honor of the Queen, by using such phrases as "the quiet of the good and the corruption of the bad, the stay of the rich and the relief of the poor, the advance of the public profit, and the restraint of injurious and private gain."

To mention injurious and private gain in that era of freebooters and holders of monopolies on necessary commodities would be tantamount to criticizing the system by which Queen Elizabeth's great peers conducted their extravagant way of life. Lambarde could of course if called before the Star Chamber defend his phrase as a means of being on the side of the jurors, a mere device to arouse them to cooperate. On the other hand, he meant it. In contrast to the petty pilfering of the poor wretches he was examining from week to week, the advantage taken of the public profit by the great peers of the land made a mockery of justice. And his phrase "the quiet of the good" emphasized the right of decent persons to live with assurance that evil persons would be found out and punished to preserve the peace.

With all his integrity and with his intent to see that justice prevailed for the deserving poor who worked hard at honest labor, Lambarde could not tolerate the extravagances of the courtiers. If ever he had been offered a knighthood, he probably would have rejected it. His principles were set against display of any kind in dress, games, food, and drink. But for all of his apparent humility, he nevertheless had a fearless attitude toward those in power who acted beyond the law with special privileges and arrogance. Human dignity, he kept repeating, belonged to rich and poor alike. But he was not sentimental about either the rich or the poor in idleness.

Then came his marriage to Sylvestria Dean Dalison on October 28, 1583, and he moved into Halling Palace with an excess of delight in both Sylvestria and the palace. She evidently was good-natured, and the palace was for him an appropriate place to live. He was the kind of man who had already demonstrated deep interest in historic places, and he seemed to have genuine affection for Halling Palace as well as for Sylvestria.

His halcyon years now reached the zenith of his enjoyment of life, and for the first time in his life he appeared to relax for a few months without his overwhelming compulsion to be at work. He heard and bound over a few routine cases. Then on December 4 he bound over two widows in the town of Shorne who were quarreling in public; he required of them ten pounds to keep the peace. He bound over to the Easter quarter sessions Thomas Alleyn and his son, who lived in Cliffe. While with William Lewyn, another justice, he ordered that Margaret Dutton be whipped at Gravesend and then sent to the House of Correction. She and Robert Cole, the father "as it is thought," who was also committed, were bound over to the Easter sessions, evidently by order of Lord Cobham and Mr. Sommer, justice of the peace.

Lambarde had traveled to three towns that December, Shorne, Cliffe, and Gravesend, and thus was truly a justice on horseback, working alone, carrying out orders, and serving with a local justice.

During his second year in Halling Palace, Lambarde gained recognition and had many new experiences. Probably now, too, Lord Cobham saw him more frequently and began to take an interest in him. He began his work this year with a curious case on January 6 when he took bail for the appearance of Loane and Garret at the next jail delivery; this pair had driven off some sheep belonging to John Lorymer of Gillingham and then sold the sheep. This was of course a very serious offense with a penalty of death. Lambarde could have determined the case at once, but he chose to postpone decision until the jail delivery.

Since the justices of the peace in Kent frequently worked in pairs, Lambarde, according to his "Ephemeris," became associated with a large number of different persons as he traveled around the division for which Lord Cobham himself assumed responsibility. Lord Cobham's name appears rather rarely in "Ephemeris," although he as Lord Lieutenant of the shire was in charge of all the Kentish justices of the peace, in particular of the Western Division in which Lambarde participated. Hence it seems likely that in traveling so widely Lambarde was acting in many of these instances as Cobham's deputy. When another distinguished person of ancient lineage, such as Lord Abergavenny, requested Lambarde's attention, there is some significance in these associations, for Lord Abergavenny might be expected to dispatch a courier to Lord Cobham who then directed Lambarde on January 7 and 10 to take charge: first, to bind over Peter Hatcher of Wrotham to appear at the next jail delivery to answer to the death of Francis Wastness, and second, to examine Lord Abergavenny's charge of John Bristoe with burglary. In the latter instance, Mr. Bing, another justice of the peace, was present to examine these charges and make out the warrant for Bristoe's commitment.

At the jail delivery he certified the examination of various persons; he released Peter Hatcher, suspected of murder by request of Lord Abergavenny, who had had the man committed. He also released Loane and Garret, charged with stealing sheep and selling them, on the opinion of Sir Thomas Gawdy, judge of Assize, who found in fact no felony.

At this time he was appointed to the Commission of Oyer and Terminer, which supplemented the work of the judges of Assizes and therefore was an extension of the King's Court in Westminister. On the local scene, Lambarde's authority became very inclusive, and this appointment gave official status to the work that he had already been doing for the judges of Assizes on individual assignments, particularly with reference to Sir Thomas Gawdy, who indeed might have been responsible for Lambarde's extended authority. On the other hand, Lord Cobham was a Privy Councillor and had the power to recommend Lambarde's advancement as a jurist to hear and determine civil cases as well as the criminal cases beyond the jurisdiction of the justices of the peace. Hence a little more than three years after his appointment to the Commission of the Peace, he had become established as the principal judge within the limits of Kent. There was no question of his preeminent learning. He had demonstrated his interest by diligent service, and now he merited the recognition that superior persons in the hierarchy of the judicial could give him.

Still he was involved in such matters as licensing, with Lord Cobham, an alehouse at the "Sign of the George," near the church stile. In retrospect, it seems that such work might have been done by persons with less to do than Lord Cobham and Lambarde. He also continued with routine cases. Then on March 14 he discharged a woman named Abigail from the House of Correction, after receiving promises from two men and her mother-in-law that she would be taken into "honest service." On March 20 with William Lewyn he ordered the whipping of Alice Trammel of Cliffe for having a bastard. During the next days he bound over several husbandmen, laborers, and yeomen to keep the peace to the next quarter sessions, and he also sent to jail a man for burglary and a woman for stealing. With Sir Thomas Fane he released a man held on suspicion of felony; evidently Fane had been knighted since last he served with Lambarde. Nearly all the important jurists were knighted, and one wonders why Lambarde was overlooked.

He certified the various recognizances at the quarter sessions held on April 18 and had evidently prepared a Charge to the Jurors, which for some reason he did not utter.

At this time, rumors of the sailing of the Spanish Armada and false reports of French troops landing in Ireland, Wales, or along some beach in England were being circulated throughout the country. Lambarde's "Ephemeris" reveals how seriously such murmurings influenced the Privy Council four years before the great Armada sailed. On May 6, 1584, the Privy Council gave instructions for Thomas Churchyard to meet with the High Sheriff and Commission for Musters. At this time the High Sheriff in Kent was Justinian Champneys. The purpose of this meeting was to nominate the captains for troops, to be chosen from the sons of the principal gentlemen of the county. Lambarde listed the names of the persons on the Commission for Musters: the knights were Thomas Scott, Thomas Fane, Edward Hobby; the gentlemen were John Cobham, William Crowmer, Thomas Willoughby, Edward Boyse, John Sommer, William Partridge, William Lambarde, and Henry Palmer. Several of these men had served with Lambarde as justices of the peace. Thomas Churchyard was authorized to select and train 4,000 men.

Lambarde conducted the jail delivery at Rochester on July 13. This responsibility formerly was reserved for the High Sheriff in conjunction with the judges of Assize.

When Lambarde released Margaret Dutton from the House of Correction, on July 26, 1584, an interesting condition was that a man named Robert Startop undertook to keep her in service for a whole year. The assumption was that this disorderly woman had been rehabilitated during her stay in the House of Correction and could therefore give promise of being a useful servant. If this assumption was valid, then Kentish justices had accomplished much with their pioneer work in establishing the House of Correction.

At the quarter sessions on September 22, he certified as usual the various recognizances. At this time he noted "I released . . ." Formerly he had used "We," and this use of "I" was probably an indication of his increased authority as a jurist. This attitude became recognizable in his Charges to the Jurors henceforth, and it is interesting to watch this development.

The birth of his son and heir on October 15, 1584, caused much rejoicing. He named the child Multon, *"in gratia soceris mei amantissimi Georgii Multoni."* He might have used another word than "soceris," meaning father-in-law, for his most beloved friend. But this relationship he had emphasized in notations in his "Ephemeris," repeating "my father-in-law and I" many times. Surely it was not a recollection of Jane Multon, but if it had been a reminder to George Multon of the grandchild he never had, it would have made no difference to Sylvestria, if she had bothered to think of it. Multon was now a very old man, and if this baby boy could bring him any happiness, Sylvestria would in her generous and affectionate way wish to share her own happiness over the birth of her son.

During October and November Lambarde attended only one case and bound the culprit over to Easter quarter sessions; he did, however, appoint Reignold Hawke to be constable at Sharnole, when the officer in that place left. Even on the last day of December, when the accusation was made that Marjorie Tailford was with child by her master, Robert

Crips of Meopham, Lambarde merely bound the alleged culprits to the Easter quarter sessions.

One interesting feature of the authority of the justices became apparent on January 2, 1585, when the newly appointed constable, John Hawke, brought two rogues from other counties to Lambarde, one from Yorkshire, the other from Lincolnshire; Lambarde sent them both to jail. The next day, with Mr. Fludd, another justice of the peace, he took bail from several persons accused of robbery. On February 23 he sent a man and woman to jail for pilfering. Here were three cases in which persons were committed to jail and not bound over to the quarter sessions. And at the Assizes held in Rochester, on February 25, he certified all these cases and recognizances, probably an indication of the extension of his authority as of the Commission of Oyer and Terminer.

His next Charge to the Jurors at the quarter session on April 20 indicated increasing discernment of the jurors' problems and greater effort on his part to explain their part in the maintenance of justice. He took the theme of obedience and examined it from the jurors' view, manifested in their oaths, and then from the culprits' view, apparent in their boldness in breaking the law. Again he declared that felonies were primarily sins in the eyes of God, and not merely crimes against the government. If people wasted their substance on apparel, alehouses, lewd living, and unlawful games, then the strength of the nation itself must decline to weakness. For the nation, he said, was like a tree with its branches stricken so that the sap could not nourish it. Self-indulgence, irresponsibility, and desire for various pleasures could not be afforded when the nation faced disaster. Now was the time for obedience to the law, but people continued to disobey the law and even the jurors did not do their duties. They allowed their neighbors and friends to escape the penalties by not reporting felonies and misdemeanors to the justices.

Meanwhile Lambarde's old and good friend Ralph Rokeby, now a Master in the prerogative Court of Requests as well as Master of St. Catherine's, was receiving numerous assignments from the Privy Council to interrogate recusants and strangers. The great fear of infiltration by the enemy, especially of an uprising from within the nation, had led to this seeking out of recusants, seminarians, and priests. These investigations were based on the absence of strangers from church, at which attendance was required. Judging by the large number of such orders from the Privy Council, Rokeby must have devoted nearly all of his days to such work. Hence Lambarde's being assigned by the Privy Council to undertake these investigations in Maidstone, with the assistance of the local bailiffs, might have been on Rokeby's recommendation. For the Privy Council, despite Lambarde's growing reputation, would act on someone's suggestion, not of its own initiative, in this matter. Advancement by merit followed a rigid pattern of having a friend in court. Or, it is also possible that Lord Cobham or Sir Thomas Gawdy, with whom Lambarde had been associated in the Assizes, might have suggested Lambarde as the proper person to carry on these inquiries, as the threat of the Spanish Armada approached reality.

In the midst of these exciting times, Lambarde wrote a letter to Lord Burghley, advocating the support of the gentry in the drawn-out war in the lowlands. This letter, dated July 18, 1585, was Lambarde's only venture into international politics, but it revealed much of his true nature as well as the view of a man removed from the problems harassing the Privy Councillors and the Queen. For Her Majesty had many years before, in 1579, lent the low countries money from her own purse. The Earl of Leicester had led a less than brilliant campaign to no avail, and the Dutch had lost interest, meanwhile, in repaying Elizabeth's loan.

Now in June some commissioners had come from the low countries to seek further aid against the intrigues of Henry III of France and Philip II of Spain. So Lambarde, recognizing that the Queen was weary of the cost of this war, now advocated a diversionary tactic, to be undertaken with funds raised from the nobility and gentry, without touching Her Majesty's coffers. This enterprise, he thought, would lead other Protestant countries to support a bold attack upon the Roman Catholic forces.

In one passage in his very long letter to Lord Burghley, he wrote that he had told Her Majesty several things which had proved to be true, but "I have had Cassandra's luck." Now he prayed God to open Her Majesty's eyes and strengthen her heart to this bold declaration.

He dared to criticize the Queen for her failure to recognize her friends abroad and then to temporize with her enemies. As a result there was no commerce. The gentleman would be unable to sell his wool, the plowman his grain, the brazier his ware, and the unemployed artificer would cause unrest that would shake the frame of the whole state. Lambarde knew the "murmuring of all sorts," the whispering, conspiring, and exclaiming against the government, as no Privy Councillor could reflect the temper of the common people. But if the Queen could be persuaded to take bold action against her enemies, then the people would rally to her cause.

As it turned out, Lambarde was far from wrong in his bold proposal to make war openly against England's conniving enemies. The commissioners gained agreement and the treaty for the relief of Antwerp was signed on August 2; Antwerp fell five days later. The Queen then ordered the Earl of Leicester with 6,000 foot soldiers and 1,000 on horseback into action. The Battle of Zutphen cost the life of the brilliant and young Sir Philip Sidney, but gained nothing, as the Queen's temporizing with the enemy continued.

During these eventful days in August, Lambarde was hearing routine cases with Lord Cobham almost daily and binding over and taking sureties until the next quarter sessions. The contrast between important events and the business of maintaining the peace in the villages and towns of a nation in crisis emphasizes Lambarde's particular insight into foreign affairs from the countryman's point of view.

During September he heard two cases of robbery and at the quarter sessions on September 28, he certified these recognizances. Now he began serving with another justice of the peace, Mr. Leveson, rather than Lord Cobham, on a series of cases. He sent John Maunsel to the House of Correction because this local glover was the father of a bastard, the mother being a widow in the town of Strode. He sent James Tonsett to jail for burglary and bound Timothy Chudder to give evidence on surety of £20. On suit of Thomas Newman he had bound Timothy Chudder £20, William Rolfe £10, and John Hote £10, all of Higham, to appear at the Easter quarter sessions; then he apparently gained some additional information and released them all.

In the midst of rumors that the Spaniards were prepared to invade England, that the Pope had yielded to Olivarez's petitions and consequently had pledged a million crowns to help the Spaniards to invade England, there was a crop failure .The scarcity of grain added to the people's fears and privation. Some farmers, hopeful of receiving higher prices for their grain, withheld it from the market; others merely sought to preserve sufficient seed and food for themselves, but hoarded more than was necessary. On the other hand, there were many greedy men who seized this opportunity to speculate by buying up grain and keeping it from the market. The result was, of course, exorbitant prices for bread, which led to the undernourishment of countless innocent poor persons. So, at the command of the Queen, the Privy Council issued orders that the justices hold special commissions to inquire into the scarcity of grain.

In this distressing period, Lambarde's second child was born on January 8, 1586, a daughter named Margaret. Again he was overcome with joy. As with the advent of his son and heir, Multon, he accepted this second miracle of birth with deep thankfulness. The boy was now progressing sturdily in childhood, but this infant daughter seemed to evoke a sentimental feeling of responsibility for her helplessness, like any other baby, as he regarded in his imagination the child growing into womanhood.

Lambarde conducted the inquiry held at Frinsbury, January 29, 1586, and he gave the Charge to the Jurors, who on this occasion had only one responsibility: to report who was withholding grain in their respective neighborhoods. He began by reminding them that for twenty-eight years God had granted a plenteous store of food. But during these years of plenty in the realm, while the people enjoyed unprecedented peace and tranquility, they seemed unmindful of God's beneficence; at least there was slight evidence of their thankfulness to God. So the present famine, Lambarde asserted, might be God's punishment for their ingratitude.

He then added another assumption. Food was provided for the sustenance of the people, not as a means of unsatiated avarice. Many of these humble jurors were farmers eager to receive a higher rate of return from the grain that they had labored to produce. Raising grain was simply their means of livelihood, and Lambarde knew that well. Yet he continued to warn them that they must bring to market any surplus that they had stored, as well as report the greedy persons who had come into the countryside to buy grain for the purpose of withholding it from the market. Here indeed was a difficult situation for the juror who had sold his grain at higher price to a speculator than he could have received for it in the marketplace. If he revealed the purchaser, then he himself might be regarded as an accessory. Lambarde apparently recognized that at this assembly he was attempting a much more difficult task than merely bringing in felons from the various neighborhoods. So he addressed his remarks to the great hardship caused by these persons seeking to gain profit from their withholding of grain.

He continued to hear many routine cases but simply bound over the persons involved to the Easter quarter sessions. He licensed another alehouse and then committed a woman to jail for killing her child. But even in this serious crime, alleged murder, he made no determination and delayed the punishment. On April 12, he likewise sent a man to jail for killing "his wench." In both instances he called in the coroner to prepare a report, but the punishment to be meted out to these murderers he simply left to the quarter sessions. In contrast to his immediate orders for severe whippings of persons who had bastards, he now reserved punishment until after trial by jury.

He certified the various recognizances at the Assizes at Rochester on February 21 and at the quarter sessions after Easter; and at this latter assembly, he gave the Charge to the Jurors. He referred definitely to the increase in murders: how idleness led to robbery, bastardy, and all manner of felonies that must be sought out by the jurors lest these evildoers set a bad example to the jurors' sons and servants. Treason, too, was much on his mind, as he referred to witchcraft and popery as means to overthrowing the government and the true religion which the jurors professed but apparently were careless of protecting.

Keeping of these official records and writing out the necessary orders for the court officer, even though he employed a scribe, required much attention from this conscientious justice. With reports to the judges in Westminister and the Privy Councillors, Lambarde had become the chief administrator of local justice in Kent.

The way local government functioned is revealed in an interesting case on July 17. After he had received information from Matthew Bridges, a gentleman from Denton, that Joan Myles had stolen apparel from Paul Baker in the Old Bailey prison of London, Lambarde used a local borsholder as the officer to convey the prisoner and the records of the case to London, and also bound over Bridges to give evidence at the Newgate prison in London. The development of this case by testimony taken in Kent rather than by a writ issuing from a London court, concerning a felony committed in London, indicates how alleged culprits were treated in these perilous times.

By the spring of 1586 excitement was mounting in the hearts and minds of the people. The dullest oaf going through his daily routine listened to the gossip that Jesuit emissaries and seminary priests were hiding in the homes of recusants ready to lead the counterreformation against the English church. It was rumored that there were foreign soldiers lurking in the alehouses, harbingers of the invasion and the coming of the Spaniards in their high-masted galleons. And no doubt some persons were making the most of the fear that there would be a shortage of food by buying and hoarding grain to sell at higher prices and thus pocketing a few extra shillings as they traveled from farm to farm. The scarcity of food, however, was not entirely the fault of these individual speculators but was rather the result of bad weather, which was reducing production of crops and the hopes of a good harvest later on. So it was a propitious time for the common people to fall prey to the intrigues of strangers who were evident in many communities throughout Kent and other counties.

The Privy Council, taking cognizance of all these confusing reports, issued orders to the justices of the peace to make personal house-to-house inspections of all the people living in Deptford, Greenwich, Lewisham, Altham, Lye, Charlton, and Woolwich to seek out strangers and identify persons who were withholding grain from the normal trade in these market towns. This tedious work for the already overworked justices revealed that the grand jurors, or the inquirers, as Lambarde called them, in the quarter sessions and special assemblies, had not reported what was happening in their respective districts. Doubtless some of the jurors themselves had made a few extra pennies and consequently had no taste for the bitter duty of informing on neighbors and friends.

The picture of the scholarly and dignified Lambarde prowling around laborers' cottages, asking questions and poking behind closed doors, shows how close to panic was the fear of invasion. (In retrospect this procedure could only have lowered the prestige and reduced the respect due to the office of justice of the peace.) Yet there cannot be any doubt that Lambarde believed that this procedure was necessary. It is difficult to extract from the times any more significant insight into the state of England in the spring of 1586, when fears, rumors, and scarcity of grain for bread and ale touched the daily lives of both the government and the common people.

Later the same spring the Privy Council issued an order to Ralph Rokeby, Master of St. Catherine's, and William Lambarde, counselor at law, to end and compound with justice and equity the case of Dorothy Kelke, an orphan, who was defrauded of part of her legacy by Richard Foulke. The means used to defraud the girl was a false will made by the girl's brother, who was an apprentice to Foulke. This case indicated that again Rokeby was involved in bringing Lambarde to the attention of the Privy Council by asking for assistance in a case in which the facts had been determined. A curious feature was the designation of Lambarde as "counselor at law," rather than as justice of the peace or of the Commission of Oyer and Terminer, probably so indicated at Rokeby's recommendation. Nevertheless Lambarde was a barrister and an associate of the bench of Lincoln's Inn. Evidently Rokeby was seeking to establish Lambarde as a learned colleague who should be advanced to a position commensurate with his distinction as a counselor at law. (One could suspect that Lord Chancellor Bromley had not yet forgotten Lambarde's pointing out the inaccuracies in the Commission of the Peace.)

Another indication of the dramatic tensions within the realm was the response given to the ordinance, issued by the Court of Star Chamber, requiring the licensing of all printed matter. The Privy Council had been moved to this act by Archbishop Whitgift, who was proving himself to be no middle-of-the-road churchman like his predecessor, Archbishop Parker. Whitgift wanted to stop the printing or dissemination of Presbyterian pamphlets. On the other hand, printed books and pamphlets expounding Roman Catholic doctrine were appearing surreptitiously in sufficient number to be a threat to the English church. Whitgift, already nettled by the recusants, was having difficulty with independent thinkers within his own church. But this measure was severe and abrogated the people's rights to a free press. The ordinance provided that the Archbishop and the Bishop of London, or their deputies, determine what books might be printed.

The response to this ordinance was manifested in numerous pamphlets of a boisterous temper in ridicule of ecclesiastical hierarchy and clerical dignity. This was the beginning of the famous Martin Marprelate tracts, named after the signature on many of them but augmented by other writers. These pamphlets satirized and derided the arrogant display of ecclesiastical power, as these writers viewed the ordinance, and in particular attacked Archbishop Whitgift as the instigator of this curb to free expression.

In July the Privy Council ordered the Lord Lieutenants in the various shires to muster the home guard. These guards were to be trained in the use of the harquebus and were to be stationed in strategic places to keep night watches, prepare beacons for spreading the alarm, seek out foreign priests, and arrest any persons who disturbed the peace with false rumors. Evidently the house-to-house visitation of the justices had not found nearly all the seminarians and priests, since it seemed necessary for the home guard to participate in the hunt.

The Privy Council furthermore ordered the justices to hear and determine all manner of cases involving treason, heresy, and witchcraft and to report these matters immediately to Sir Francis Walsingham and the Privy Council. Since Sir Francis already had a large and efficient, though costly, group of informers and investigators, the pressing into service of the local justices now emphasized the high state of fear permeating the government. As rumors flooded Sir Francis Walsingham's office, notices were dispatched to the justices to investigate, while Walsingham's men followed to discover what the justices had determined. These were then the conditions under which Lambarde charged the jurors with increasingly sharply worded threats.

Local tensions kept pace with the pressures felt by the Privy Councillors. The common people continued to become increasingly involved in serious and petty crimes as the nation prepared to repel invasion. Order was dislocated to such an extent that it was extremely difficult for the justices, now burdened with extra duties, to maintain strict surveillance of the local scene.

On January 10, 1587, Lambarde bound over a widow in Halling and two yeomen to be of good behavior until the quarter sessions; on the 19th, he was associated with Fane, Sedley, and Becher, various justices of the peace, in taking bail of a cook and two yeomen until the next jail delivery. The increased number of bindings over instead of the decisive ordering of punishments would seem to indicate that the justices had established this procedure because they had too many other duties; at this time they could scarcely pause after their hearings to form decisions and see that their orders were carried out. As a result, however, the calendars of the quarter sessions and jail deliveries became excessively full for the time allotted to these assemblies.

Meanwhile Lambarde's friend Rokeby was knighted and Lambarde wrote to him about a case that required relief from the Masters in the Court of Requests. He described himself and Sylvestria as the widower and widow of Halling, probably thus designating their official responsibility in the care of the parish poor. His letter concerned the loss of a legal paper that required certain wealthy persons to support a poor family in the parish. With the loss of the legal paper, the benefactors had stopped giving relief. Lambarde consequently was sending the poor petitioners to Rokeby for a court order to continue their support; he even cited the statute relevant to the case and interpreted it for Rokeby: namely, that regardless of the fact that the instrument was lacking, the relief should continue.

At this time Lambarde received a letter from Lady Jane Fitzjames requesting clemency for Michael Eliot, a servant who had stolen a serving spoon. She insisted that the young man was sorry for this, his first offense. Lambarde merely endorsed the letter: "Lady Fitzjames, touching Michael

Eliot, a felon, 1587." Lambarde could have released the servant to the custody of Lady Fitzjames, but he doubtless felt that Eliot had appealed to the lady's emotions and deserved punishment as an example to other servants; that would be indicated by his designation that despite Lady Jane's petition, Michael Eliot was a felon.

On February 8, 1587, Mary Queen of Scots was beheaded by order of the Privy Council. Lambarde's old friend Sir Thomas Egerton had distinguished himself as the prosecutor in her trial, by giving a calm presentation of facts without emotional pyrotechnics. As day by day the tensions had mounted among the Privy Councillors, however, they had feared Queen Mary as a Roman Catholic perhaps more than as a possible successor to Queen Elizabeth; rumor of Mary's alliance with the Roman Catholics of France and Spain caused the peers of the realm, confronted with the impending invasion by the Spaniards, to seek every means to block internal uprising. And their fears were fully substantiated by those of the Members of Parliament; everyone wanted some kind of action during this tense period of waiting for the Spaniards to strike.

Following the dissolution of Parliament on March 27, Lambarde gave the Charge to the Jurors at the quarter session after Easter. The gravity of the national situation was combined for Lambarde with personal anxiety for Sylvestria, who was pregnant and ill.

In this state of mind he addressed the jurors. He carefully analyzed the failure of the jury system. The "inquiring" jurors had repeatedly failed to seek out the enemy at home; they investigated only those cases referred to them, and since they represented various parts of the shire they were the "eyes to discover evildoers" and report them. His second point was that fear of revenge by persons of high rank caused the jurors to remain quiet about the evil deeds of "their betters." Lest some powerful persons should become offended or angry, the jurors remained silent. Hence they broke their oaths, taken in the sight of God, and revealed themselves as more fearful of mortal men than of God. A third group of jurors, he said, were unwilling to present evidence against their enemies and thus, by means of malice and hatred, these jurors prevented justice from being attained as much as those who remained silent. He spoke with intensity and sharpness, reminding them that his demands of them amounted to the decision of survival for them and the nation.

In this eventful year of 1587 Sir Thomas Bromley died, and Queen Elizabeth quickly appointed Sir Christopher Hatton as Lord Chancellor. Hatton came to office in England's fateful hour and, though he was not highly regarded by his peers as a lawyer, he had tact and intelligence beyond most men, and he had genius for getting men to work together with common purpose. He was like Sir Charles Howard, the Admiral of the Fleet, who was able to bring together such individuals as Sir Francis Drake, Sir John Hawkins, and Sir Martin Frobisher. Hatton could gain support from John Whitgift, the Archbishop of Canterbury; the great Lord Burghley; Sir Charles Howard; and Lord Hunsdon, the Lord Chamberlain, in charge of the land forces. And this was an hour for leadership by men like Hatton and Howard, who perhaps lacked nearly all the talents required in their important posts, except the supreme ability of gaining cooperation among men who had the necessary skills in abundance.

On June 23, 1587, Lambarde observed that thirteen of the fifty men from Lathe of Aylesford had been outfitted and given money; Kent was to outfit three hundred soldiers for the defense of the island kingdom.

During the late summer Lambarde received a letter from Audrey Multon, his sister-in-law, addressing him as "good brother" and asking for his intercession with his good friend

Ralph Rokeby, who was of course Master in the Court of Requests. She was writing in behalf of her husband's uncle, who, she thought, was suffering a great financial loss because of a "cunning adversary." But why did not young George Multon himself write about his uncle's problem? As the brother of Lambarde's first wife possibly he resented Lambarde's remarriage. Or had some estrangement arisen between these brothers-in-law over the settlement of the elder Multon's estate? On the other hand, Audrey knew little of court procedure and from the goodness of her heart wanted to do something for George's uncle. Remembering that Ralph Rokeby was one of Lambarde's close friends, she followed her impulse by writing to her brother-in-law. In closing this very friendly letter, she referred to Lambarde's second wife as "Mrs. Dean," not as "your wife," or as "Mrs. Lambarde." So it might have been that Lambarde's remarriage had not pleased the Multons; nevertheless Audrey signed her letter, "Your loving sister much loved, Audrey Multon."

Late in August, 1587, Sylvestria gave birth to twin boys, and Lambarde promptly named them after two of his friends, Fane and Gore. He had served on many hearings and determinations with his fellow justice Sir Thomas Fane. Sir John Gore, who was approximately the same age as Ralph Rokeby, was another old friend of Lincoln's Inn, for whose knowledge of the law Lambarde had great respect. But Sylvestria did not recover her strength and died on September 1.

Lambarde forthwith decided to commemorate her motherhood with a prominent but rather modest brass panel in the Halling church. On the west pillar near the north wall, this panel, wrought in bold relief, depicted Sylvestria lying in a large four-poster bed, as if asleep; the two older children of her first marriage appeared on the far side of the bed and in the foreground are Multon, Margaret, and Fane and Gore in a double cradle. Tastes in these matters would change through the years, but Lambarde's affection and purpose in erecting this brass panel representing motherhood could not ever be misunderstood; he had loved this pretty and buxom woman with all his heart.

The sudden death of Sylvestria affected Lambarde's residing in Halling Palace. Its title had passed to her son Maximilian, who at thirteen years of age came under the protection of the Court of Wards. As a result of this normal, if unexpected, situation, Lambarde and his small children—his three-year-old heir, his daughter almost two, and the infant twins—were required by law to seek domicile elsewhere. Such a turn in the affairs of a lawyer whose reputation for tenure of land in Kent was second to none might seem thoroughly ironic. Of all persons marrying widows, he should have foreseen this possible outcome. However, despite his obvious delight in living in Halling Palace, he had fallen in love with a widow half his age; his expectation might have been that she would survive him. As a matter of fact he might have known that with her marriage to Dalison this lease passed to him; on his death to his son Maximilian in 1581; and Sylvestria had only her moiety, or widow's dower, in the property. Hence it seems that Lambarde could have done nothing about the situation at the time of his marriage to Sylvestria.

Now he did something about it. After consultation with Lord Cobham, he wrote directly to the great Lord Burghley, whose power extended beyond his office as the Lord Treasurer. Burghley arranged for Lambarde to remain in Halling. Four days after the death of Sylvestria, he wrote to Burghley about the "pity of his estate" and "my poor sucklings" to give his thanks for granting his "desire presented on my behalf by that my favorable and father-like good Lord Cobham." This was indeed rapid action in response to his "petitions." He also dramatized his pitiable estate on his "farm in Halling"—not Halling Palace, but a "farm." Lambarde's modesty at times became self-depreciating.

During the remainder of 1587, except for the month of November, Lambarde continued to hear and determine cases as a justice of the peace. These times were not for prolonged mourning, although his grief and frustration were evidently very great indeed, augmented, no doubt, by his responsibility of caring for four very small children. On September 14, he heard how a man named Russell, a Scot, had become involved with Rebecca Gore of East Malling. He sent for the girl's father but "Old Gore" had disappeared. So he ordered the appearance of James Dowle, the local borsholder, evidently to turn over to him the details of this case. Here was local government grinding out justice, not in theory but with all the complications of human relationships. Such was the experience and understanding that Lambarde brought to *Eirenarcha*.

He bound over a loader, farm helper, for stealing wheat from his master and bound over a witness to give evidence; this occurred on October 2. Then in December he sent two minstrels to the House of Correction rather than to jail, an interesting use of that institution. They were to spend only six days, apparently to be dismissed in time for Christmas. On December 10, he bound over a butcher, a tailor, and a yeoman to keep the peace until Shrove Sunday, and sent Thomas Smith of Malling to jail for counterfeiting money and stealing, binding over several witnesses to give evidence against this man.

On December 19, Lambarde wrote a long letter to Sir Thomas Egerton, Her Majesty's solicitor. This letter accompanied a Christmas gift of a manuscript, a copy Lambarde had made of Fitz-Neal's "Dialogue of the Exchequer," called "Gervasius, surnamed Tylberie in Essex, over against Gravesend." He apologized for the errors made by his copyist, although he himself had amended it and added to it "in red ink"; he also had made a table for easy reference. This letter, written from Halling, seems to imply that Egerton had assisted in whatever arrangements had to be made for Lambarde's continued residence in Halling, as indicated in the letter the previous September to Lord Burghley. The gratitude that Lambarde expressed thus to Egerton, as well as the magnificent gift, indicated more than common favors bestowed upon him by Egerton. The letter contains certain phrases of graceful wit concerning the reading of the book as like a game of chess, in which the speakers of the dialogues discuss the Exchequer:

> I send you Gervasius, surnamed of Tylberie in Essex over against Gravesend, with whome you may (if it please you) now and then play a game at Chestes, (for so he calleth all that which he handeleth in theise Dialogues, and observations of the Excheaquer) in this Christmas tyme, when other men be occupied at Dyce and Cardes, and that with lesse losse, and no less pleasure, then the tyme is passed by theim.

His apologies for the workmanship of the copyist were combined with his evident expectation that Egerton would find profit and pleasure in the book:

> Sorry I am, that I have not a better Copie for you, and (which is worse) that I have not, nor ever had, a man that could do it better for me. And yet I must acknowledge, that I have reaped some fruite in my tyme by evel writing of bookes, which (if I had mett withall in good Letters, or prynte), would have escaped me.

The moving feature of this letter was the quiet loneliness of this man, almost a tragic figure, reaching out for friendship as he manifested his warm regard for an old friend with a choice gift. He must have felt even in his loneliness some satisfaction as he learned that three persons during the year had made bequests to the endowment of his College for the Poor of Queen Elizabeth. Joan Tallis, Peter Wotton, and Dennis Charpel had ordered in their wills that variant sums of money be given to Lambarde's College. Since these items have been preserved only by chance, there might indeed have been other tokens of approval for his farsighted establishment of a place of refuge for the weak and afflicted poor.

These private matters have significance, a rather universal application, beyond the experience of William Lambarde. In every period of national crisis, when the defense of a nation, even the existence of the nation, becomes primary, only a few persons, such as the aircraft pilots in the Battle of Britain in World War II, bear the armor against the enemy. So it was then: the officers and sailors aboard the *Ark Royal*, the *Bonaventure*, or the *Revenge* were the persons to confront the enemy at sea against overwhelming odds, while the army prepared to fight on the beaches and plains in Kent. But the mass of people went about their daily chores, being too old or too young, or unfit physically or for lack of training, to bear arms against the invaders.

In the concentrated view of history, there is no space for recording the experiences of men not directly involved in the main issue. What the people were doing has remained of little concern and mattered, obviously, much less than the preparation of earthen works to withstand the waves of assault, the maintenance of the beacons fed by wood fires to signal the ships at sea and to alert the defenders, and the placing of troops in strategic positions near the shores.

Lambarde's experiences reveal that even in the most crucial times, the people, the soldiers, and the sailors continued to steal, rape, and quarrel among themselves as in times of peace, though perhaps even more so in the displacement of persons in this preparation for war. No day passed without rumors that the Spaniards had been sighted at sea or had landed along the shore. Maintenance of the peace, some semblance of order, was more important than ever under these conditions. And Lambarde's notes showed what was happening and represented the additional duties imposed upon people who had casually gone about their routine tasks without much interest in them and now were suddenly expected to extend their efforts to produce extra food, curtail personal pleasures, and go without sleep in order to tend the important beacons throughout the night.

Whatever modicum of incentive this vast mass of human beings might have expected to hold in their labors to support the aristocracy in ordinary conditions was suddenly aroused by fear of death and rumors of what the Spaniards and the French would do to them if England was conquered. People who knew that they had no importance in the social scheme of everyday life now had a feeling of belonging to England after all, a new sense of responsibility, or perhaps only of adventure, in contrast to the dull routine of their previous existence.

In the monarchial structure of government in Elizabethan England, there were few so-called democratic vistas to give the people hope. The status quo was maintained, except for the few who had enough luck and talent to emerge from the place to which God had appointed them. So Lambarde's view of common man, even through the mist of more than 350 years, is exciting and should be recognized for its advancement of the cause of common man.

In the practical affairs of existence, Lambarde offered not abstract justice in beautiful phrases, but plain honesty in explaining and dealing with legal justice.

Chapter 6

INCREASED RESPONSIBILITIES
AND HONORS (1588–1591)

The fateful year of 1588 began in England with expectation
on the part of both government and people that the Spaniards
would surely sail their Armada in the springtime. After years
of rumors and false alarms, everyone believed that the time
of testing had come. Englishmen were braced to withstand
the onslaught of the mighty ships and the troops that would
probably land in Kent. It was not that other coastal counties
were less prepared; but Kent was the likely place because it
was there that the Norman invaders had struck, met stout
resistance, and finally landed and won the Battle of Hastings.
The residents of the Cinque Ports in particular were sharing
shelter and food with the soldiers garrisoned there and also
with the sailors from the ships that periodically entered into
these ports. Sir Charles Howard had given to each of his
famous captains, Drake, Hawkins, and Frobisher, individual
squadrons of ships large and small to patrol designated areas
of the English Channel and had coordinated their movements in guarding these areas. While on land Queen Elizabeth had accepted Leicester's importuning that she be with
him in the sight of her soldiers; the watch and ward waited

throughout England under the direction of Lord Hunsdon.

For the justices like Lambarde, hearings and determinations continued as if the nation were not about to meet the fateful decision of victory or defeat. The dislocations of trade and building, the separation of families, general unrest, and continued scarcity of food augmented the usual problems of local government. During January, Lambarde heard two cases of bastardy, sent a man to jail for stealing, and licensed a man to sell beer. He ordered four persons to be whipped in the marketplace of East Malling. And in February he conducted the jail delivery at Sevenoaks.

In the crosscurrents of national and local government at this crucial time the Crown required more revenue to meet the enormous expenditures in this final stage of preparing to resist invaders. To meet this emergency, Lord Cobham's division of the Commission of Peace, represented by Lambarde and Becher, held on March 8, at Strood Church, a most unusual assembly to order the arrearages for the composition of wheat. (This took place three years earlier, according to Lambarde's notation, than had previously been known; Kent compounded for wheat in 1591, and for other grains in 1594.[1]) This composition of wheat served two purposes: it provided revenue for the Crown and also exposed the three methods of withholding grain from its normal flow to market —namely, by regrating, forestalling, and sequestering. These technical terms described the various methods of buying up grain and storing it. And as a result of this meeting, more grain evidently became available for bread.

The justices of the peace were busy enough with local problems arising from complaints of their neighbors and friends, but under the mounting tensions of impending invasion, scarcity of grain, and investigations of persons reported by Secretary Walsingham's spies, the duties were almost unbearable. During this crisis Lambarde was also trying to revise his *Eirenarcha* for a new edition. His practical experience had adduced new material as Parliament continued to enact statutes which had to be tested. Indeed questions of treason and "misprison of treason," when a person failed to report an act, or even suspicion, of treason, became highly complicated in hearings and determinations, such as Lambarde heard at this time in Malling and West Malling.

He gave the Charge to the Jurors at the quarter sessions in Maidstone on April 16, and certified all the recognizances that had meanwhile accumulated.[2] This Charge revealed his religious faith, as he spoke more like a preacher than a jurist. He began by stating that he recognized that his remarks would not influence their standards of value, "as the minds of men were variable." Yet he hoped that they would agree with him that the love of decency must prevail over all other desires and the care of the commonwealth should be the most important concern with benefit to all. The commonwealth, like an orchard, must be trimmed of rank growth, so that the tender branches can grow in strength, herbs develop, with watering, dunging, and digging so that an increased yield will be produced.

He stressed the concept of ideal justice that the good should be rewarded and evil punished. For if evil manners and customs were allowed to continue unreported, the jurors failed in their husbandry of the commonwealth. He reminded them of the benefits that they derived from a "free and unfearable administration of law and justice."

The second edition of *Eirenarcha* appeared in 1588 with the first part revised but with the original second part now expanded into three parts.[3] (This is the form usually referred to by historians.) The new second part greatly elaborated upon the various kinds of causes, and included application of the new statutes and ordinances, on which the justice had authority to act alone. The third part dealt with similar elaboration upon the authority and duties of two or more justices acting together, and the fourth part dealt with the procedures for conducting the quarter sessions.

Although no action had been taken on Lambarde's strictures on the errors in the Commission of 1580, he, nevertheless, now wrote with increased authority from his experience of almost eight years in active service as a justice; he showed no hesitancy in giving opinions and detailed directions. Thus this 1588 edition was much more than an expanded book to accommodate the large number of additional statutes and ordinances under the jurisdiction of the justices. It was a totally new book. For example, Lambarde declared that the oaths of all the justices were "dirigible," or directed to, the justices alone and should be taken only in the quarter sessions. There were many features in this new edition that strengthened the work of the justices by explaining to them in more detail how to proceed, as well as educating them in the law.

On May 25, 1588, George Multon died, after a period of ill health. His death, coming at age eighty-five, could not have surprised Lambarde, but it apparently shocked him. For this man had been a father and a guide to him through his first experiences as a justice.

In the late spring of 1588, as final preparations against the coming of the Spanish Armada reached their climax, one of Lambarde's fellow justices of the peace in Kent discovered a shortage of pitch to burn in the "pitchpots," or beacons, used along the coast not only to warn English mariners from rocks and to guide them safely into harbors but also as a system of alarm for when the Armada came into view. The maintenance of these beacons had become of primary importance in Kent because of the long coastline along the English Channel. They had to be kept burning at all costs by men who did their work by day and guarded or tended the beacons by night. But now the scarcity of pitch posed a serious problem. Roger Twysden, who was in charge of the beacons, remembered reading in Lambarde's *A Perambulation of Kent* that in ancient times, as early as King Edward II, men had used great stacks of wood for this purpose. So Twysden sought in this emergency to revive this practice to supplement the waning supply of pitch.[4]

The Privy Council also directed the justices to take inventory of the iron ordnances in Suffolk and of the transport of the iron pieces to other counties; the licenses for these pieces had to be gained from the Crown. The Lord Admiral, Lord Brockhurst, and Lord Cobham were thus instructed to see that the order was carried out. Lord Cobham was also informed that he was responsible for maintaining the watch and ward throughout Kent, particularly along the coast.

Near the end of July, 1588, the Spanish Armada appeared off Plymouth, darkening the horizon with high-masted sails. Lord Howard, the Admiral of the English fleet, was waiting inside Plymouth Harbor with Sir Francis Drake. Martin Frobisher, John Hawkins, and other less famous commanders had squadrons patrolling the Channel from Plymouth to Calais. But the English were in no hurry to engage the mighty fleet directed by Medina Sidonia, who deployed his ships both large and small in a long crescent that seemed like a wooden bulwark. The English commanders avoided becoming encircled and sallied out and around the Spaniards whose great ships were even more formidable than expected. Nor were the English without respect for the daring Basques and Portuguese whose prowess in sailing stormy seas had become almost legendary. Then the gales and swift flowing tides caught the Armada at a disadvantage, and Lord Howard's strategy proved to be sound. One battle impinged upon another day after day, until by the middle of August the issue was decided by burning galleons and storm-cast ships cracking up on rocky shores. The English remained cautious, watching attempts to regroup the mighty ships of Spain, but they continued the onslaught until the victory came to them.[5]

The defeat of the long-awaited Armada evoked wonder and wild jubilation among the English at sea and on land. The victory had occurred with stunning swiftness. Lambarde surprisingly makes no mention of it in his records. No matter that the winds and the tides had contributed to the victory, the English had sailed their ships into battle, boarded, and dispersed the enemy, all that remained of the once-dreaded ships of the mighty Armada. After the long years of agitation and agonizing suspense, the people in this tight little island fortress finally had cause for rejoicing. It seemed almost incredible to them that the dreaded event had taken place and brought victory without long delay and bitter suffering. The relief from anxiety gave piquancy to their joy. Queen Elizabeth began her progresses in celebration by visiting Cobham Hall, but every alehouse had its celebration, too.

The wonderful victory brought expectation of the return to normal living and progress with the resumption of commerce and the stabilization of trade. The roads were filled with jubilant soldiers and sailors on their way home and for them a new world seemed to lie ahead. Yet the sudden release of thousands of men who had spent months and years under command made difficult their resumption of old trades and means of livelihood. Many were unwilling to return immediately to their crafts and apprenticeships and many more were content to celebrate and follow the idlers in unlawful games of chance, excessive drinking and wenching, or merely loafing. The responsibility of steady work appeared less attractive than the occasional day labor, which provided enough money to buy the pleasures of that night. So the burdens of the justices greatly increased after the victory, as they tried to restore order in time of peace.

Parliament was called into session in September, 1588, to deal with raising money and meeting the emergency presented by roving soldiers and sailors unable either to settle down or to find appropriate work. As a matter of fact, although the enemy had suffered overwhelming defeat, the old issues remained unsettled and the Spaniards and French still threatened the peace. Thoughtful men believed that another attempt at invasion would come as soon as the enemy could reorganize its forces for making war. This threat was less particularized but no less definite.

This was the theme that Lambarde took up when he charged the jurors at the quarter sessions in Maidstone on September 24. Although he made no reference to the defeat of the Spanish Armada, he advocated no relaxation of vigilance in reporting enemies already within the realm. He spoke of the numerous new laws, repeating the substance of his complaint from his newly printed *Eirenarcha:* "How many justices (think you) may now suffice (without breaking their backs) to bear so many, not loads, but stacks of statutes . . . ?" So if the jurors felt that their responsibilities were now increased, they might well consider how heavily burdened were the justices. Yet despite the increased number of laws, Lambarde could find no improvement, no development of wholesomeness; on the contrary, the increase was from "evil to worse."

He advocated an end to traffic with other nations because merchants brought home from their travels evil customs from other countries. (Here was Lambarde's most insular view presented at the time when England needed foreign trade, as he should have known from his association with the Drapers' Company in London.) But he evidently felt strongly that the soldiers, stationed for so long on the Continent in the wars in the low countries, had returned home with manners and customs that were evil. In this Charge he also attacked the Pope because he honestly regarded the entire Roman Catholic church as the chief enemy of England, and the priests, seminarians, and recusants as the enemy within England.

Despite the general unrest of the people, men of substance and goodwill maintained amenities. Lambarde sent Sir Thomas Egerton a copy of the new edition of *Eirenarcha*, with an inscription on the flyleaf. Although he had, of course, sent Egerton a copy of the first edition, this time he wrote a letter, expressing his remembrance of the many favors Egerton had done for him and hoping that this book might give him pleasure during the Christmas holidays. The letter was dated November 18, 1588, an indication that Lambarde was sending his Christmas gift a bit earlier than usual.

All autumn the highways had been crowded with wandering men, evidently unwilling to settle down. In this month the Privy Council issued letters to the Lord Mayor of London and the Master of the Rolls to be on guard against vagabonds and "other masterless men" in Middlesex, Surrey, and Kent, who might indeed wander into the City. Various justices, including Francis Alford and Lambarde, "being men of good experience and discretion," were called by the Lord Mayor, with others, for consultation on what means to employ to maintain the peace. Sir Ralph Rokeby and Sir Owen Hopton were instructed to provide accommodations for the more than three hundred soldiers from the forces of Sir John Norris and Sir Francis Drake as they moved from Kent. Lord Cobham had been instructed to supply food for these soldiers and sailors when they disembarked at Gravesend. Lambarde was named to assist in this matter, along with Sedley, his close friend. Shortly afterwards the people of Hastings appealed to Lord Cobham for relief from the heavy expenses sustained by them in providing accommodations and food for soldiers.

Lambarde seemed to have come at last to the attention of the Privy Council, for he was assigned to settle a private dispute between John Asteley, the master of Her Majesty's jewel-house, and Francis Asteley of Maidstone, concerning a right of way; and he was asked to do so as soon as possible.

Then in December occurred the decision for which Lambarde had long waited. The Privy Council issued letters to certain members of the Middle Temple, Gray's Inn, Lincoln's Inn, and the Inner Temple to consider all statutes found by them to be either unnecessary or defective, so that Her Majesty could make recommendations to the next Parliament for repeal or reform of these statutes. Lambarde was among the four designated to perform this study, and so was his old friend John Tyndall, whom he had mentioned in both editions of *Eirenarcha* as one competent to select the statutes dealing with the work of the justices; Francis Bacon was among those from Gray's Inn.

This appraisal of the statutes also signified Queen Elizabeth's interest in legal justice, earlier manifested in her order for the revision of the Commission of the Peace, which Bromley had so ineptly attempted and Lambarde had dared to criticize in his letter to Bromley. It well might be that the growing recognition of *Eirenarcha*, after several reprintings and a second edition, had finally established the full measure of Lambarde's authority; the next development would be the revision of the Commission in the light of his criticism. For his second edition of *Eirenarcha* had made the complaint of the "stacks of statutes" that were breaking the backs of the justices. This complaint had gained attention; it would follow logically that the duties of the justices must be defined more accurately.

If Lambarde's sharp words about the Pope and his emissaries in his Charge to the Jurors had seemed excessive, then the speech of the Lord Chancellor, Sir Christopher Hatton, at the opening of Parliament in February, 1589, placed Lambarde's view in proper perspective. Hatton outdid Lambarde's attack on the enemy within; namely, the infiltration of Roman Catholics from the Continent. Five months after the defeat of the Spanish Armada, the Queen called Parliament to raise money to pay the arrears on the war and to provide for the future defense. It was Hatton's task to make indubitably clear to the Members of Parliament that the enemy had suffered defeat but had not given up its objective to conquer England. It was therefore necessary to define the enemy, since the time for tolerance had passed. The great movement against England was produced and sustained by the Pope, using the envious rulers of Continental nations to recover England to Roman Catholicism. Hence it is clear that fears and intolerance were part of the time, not merely an expression of Lambarde's personal animosity.

Lambarde's gradual association with the great Lord Burghley progressed to the point of patronage. After the death of his wife on April 4, 1589, the tired statesman appeared to weaken physically. His wife's understanding had helped him to carry his incredible burden of state affairs. Although his son, Robert Cecil, had assumed of late many of these responsibilities, Burghley turned in September to Lambarde with the offer of being his deputy in the Office of Composition for the Alienations of Fines. This important office was concerned with the transfer of land by sales, leases, and alienation of tenure. In particular, however, it was a source of revenue accruing to the Crown; of especially great significance was the return of lands to the Crown through alienation of lands when the landlord was convicted of treason and heresy.

Burghley's recognition of Lambarde's learning and integrity indicated the favor of Her Majesty as well as that of her Lord Treasurer; nevertheless, Lambarde took a few days to think over this proposal and in the interim he appeared in Maidstone at the quarter sessions on September 23, 1589, to give the Charge to the Jurors. He repeated many of the exhortations and admonitions, the threats and warnings, that he had voiced many times before, but he emphasized "the common good," a concept that had become the mainstay of his thinking about justice and the maintenance of peace. He again reminded the jurors that the execution of the laws was in their care. Once more he charged that the Pope was the chief instigator of unrest. He urged the jurors to drive "his secretaries (Seminarians and Jesuits)" out of the realm.

Obviously Lambarde followed the Lord Chancellor's speech to Parliament in these drastic declarations, but he himself needed no urging from anyone to develop his favorite thesis of destroying the enemy within the realm. Statutes against the Roman Catholics were explicit: they were ministers of both treason and heresy and by necessity they concealed their identification with the Church of Rome. So Lambarde had every right to speak with intolerance against them. He admonished the jurors to recognize that their chief duty consisted of inquiring for and presenting evildoers from their neighborhoods. They were under oath to bring these culprits into the quarter sessions and to conceal no one. Whatever they had observed or heard reported from other men, any offense whatsoever against the law, was to be brought in evidence.

After the quarter sessions Lambarde returned home to reflect upon Burghley's proposal and to write his reply. It is evident from Lambarde's letter that he felt duty-bound to accept this appointment, at least for a term, but this particular assignment or honor was scarcely what he had expected. If Burghley had offered this post to him earlier in his career, when the office was instituted thirteen years before, Lambarde probably would have been pleased to accept this important office in the national government. Now he felt tired and lonely and had gained some personal satisfaction with the continuing success of *Eirenarcha* and *The Duties of Constables*. Although his years of devoted study had brought him no more than a modicum of recognition from the Privy Councillors, perhaps he thought that he had made his contribution.

His private experience in buying and selling tenements, manors, and farms to endow his College, even as late as two years before, had provided him with special knowledge and experience in such transactions. He was as well versed in the tenure of land as he was in the office of justice. But it was his deep sense of duty to Her Majesty and his personal feeling of responsibility to use his talents for the common good that evidently prompted him to accept this office.

On October 4, he wrote to Burghley and apologized for delay in replying to his letter of September 30. (Although that date might indicate the formal offer, other letters now lost, or even conversations about this matter, probably preceded the letter to which Lambarde referred.) He began by acknowledging his great indebtedness for more favors that he had received from Burghley than from all other persons alive. He also acknowledged that he had reaped "some benefit of Her Majesty (which I received from the free hand of your honour)" and consequently was doubly bound to serve Her Highness. But owing to "decay of eyesight and discontinuance of study," he asked for a period of "probation, to serve for the next term only," so that after this experience he would be able to judge whether he was "fit to discharge the trust that belongeth to that place."

This reply was characteristic of Lambarde's humility, but the letter certainly indicated his reluctance to accept the appointment. No doubt that a man who had read manuscript all his life should feel "decay of eyesight," but had he discontinued study? He certainly had not. Perhaps in a relative sense, compared to the enormous work of preparing the second edition of *Eirenarcha* some eighteen months before this, he was not at the moment so intensely engaged in study. But even now he was engaged in writing a history of the Star Chamber, perhaps his most profound analysis. Indeed, if the honor had been greater, if Burghley's offer had been a judgeship, either in a court in Westminister or in the Chancery, he perhaps would have been less reluctant to accept. But to be the Lord Treasurer's deputy in this exceedingly difficult office of ascertaining the values of the land and deciding upon the fine or pardon to be paid for the transfer of land scarcely appealed to him beyond his sense of duty.

Once he accepted the appointment, as when he was appointed to the Commission of the Peace, he began to investigate and write out the duties of the office. He later entitled his essay "Of the Service Called the Office of Composition for Alienations." A copy of this essay, entitled "Discourse of the Office for the Composition of Alienations," was found in Gray's Inn and was subsequently attributed to Francis Bacon. (The full text of the copy is available in standard editions of Bacon's *Works*.) [6]

Since the Office of Alienations had been instituted only thirteen years before Lambarde's appointment to it, learning and recording its history was not a formidable task. But he also made a complete accounting at the end of five years in office, to list all income received by his predecessors as well as by him during his two terms as deputy. When he began listing the receipts, he divided each year into four terms; and under each term he listed three categories: Writs of Covenant, License, Pardons, Entails, and Mean Rates. The concept for these revenues accruing to the Crown rested upon the ancient premise that all the land in the realm originally belonged to the sovereign. Through the centuries, however, the Crown had sold, given, or leased lands in reward for various kinds of services rendered. Thus varied kinds of land possession had developed; not only were there ancient divisions of land into sections of vast acreage, manors, and farms, but also in more recent times these parcels had been transferred from one tenant to another by sale, lease, inheritance, or gift, until there was a veritable maze of claims and counterclaims. A fee (fine or pardon) was charged for the privilege of transferring a holding from one person to another, regardless of the method; and it was for the determination of these fines that the office was instituted—that is, composition simply meant an agreement, and alienation described the kind of transfer.

It was reasonable to expect that men would try to pay the lowest fee possible for the privilege of transferring their estates, farms, or messuages. (The land on which a building could be erected was called a messuage, though the term often designated a building on such a lot.) There apparently had occurred slight change in the methods of assessing property. As Lambarde pointed out, merely to designate the number of acres did not represent the true value at all. Some land had been plowed, ditched, and fertilized, and such husbandry obviously increased the value of the land and increased its productivity. On the other hand, there were large tracts of unimproved land that yielded slight income when compared with that of the improved land. Yet for both types the fee for transfer had remained the same.

While Lambarde gained experience in these particulars, he detected another inequity in these transfers of land. Persons without either influence or money were forced to accept false evaluations because they could not afford to make complaint to the Court of Exchequer, the Chancery, or even in a lower court of common law. He found that some minor officers accepted fees to conceal the true value or the kind of alienation involved, and that other minor officers merely made mistakes through carelessness. So when he finished with his examination of these methods, he was thoroughly displeased with the way this work was done. Once again, as with the Commission of the Peace, he was organizer and reformer of methods, and he thus proceeded to write an "Act for Parliament" to correct the apparent deficiencies in the present conduct of this office. In addition to pointing out that land value should not be based entirely on acreage, but also on the degree of cultivation given it, he showed that land by the sea or near the border was especially useful to the Crown in time of war and, consequently, merited particular appraisal. If the Crown purposed to use the land for defense by either preemption or impressment, then that land should be given special treatment in the charges made against it. Furthermore, he had the courage to point out that peers, judges, and other officers of the realm received special dispensations in fees sharply contrasting to those exacted from tenants and poor persons with small plots of land. So equal justice for rich and poor alike had again become his theme.

In this "Act for Parliament" Lambarde specifically dealt with technicalities; for example, he cited the case of a pardon for which one whole year's value, together with the mean rates thereof, must be paid. (He knew this fact from his obtaining pardons for the lands used for his College.) He thought it would be more equitable to consider for the pardon a third part of one year's rent, as was the case when a license was issued, or a writ of entry, or address of covenant. He emphasized that if the conveyance was for a charitable purpose, or conveyance of land without change in possession, then the fines should be different from those in mortgages, or life estate. Finally he discussed the scribal errors in conveyances, which, once established, made procedures very confusing in determining title to a parcel of land. During this period of interruption in his writing of the essay "Of the Court called the Starre Chambre," he was nevertheless acquiring firsthand knowledge of how the work was done in the Court of the Exchequer. When he finished his essay of fifty-three manuscript pages about the Star Chamber, he signed his name and dated the manuscript 1589. Undoubtedly he sent it to Lord Burghley, as later events confirmed.

In this essay he explained how the sovereign had used this prerogative court from early times to deal swiftly with treason and heresy; likewise, riots that might be uprisings against the government could be quickly determined. The court itself, he wrote, consisted of the peers of the realm, in particular the Privy Councillors. They issued the orders for inquiries, and, after receiving these reports from competent judges, made their determinations with justice and equity. Lambarde's essay gave high praise to the Star Chamber, emphasizing the rapidity of its decisive actions to protect the realm. It would seem obvious, therefore, that after his years of experience with "inquiring jurors," who failed to seek out information and present it, he had become weary of the law's delay and the persistent problem of being unable to detect and punish culprits. Direct inquiry and summary determination in matters of high importance to the maintenance of the government required better means of detection and inquiry than jurors had provided. He could not overlook the numerous instances when his friend Ralph Rokeby had competently held hearings of persons assigned to his attention by the Privy Council for determination in the Star Chamber; Lambarde himself had engaged in such hearings and reported his finding to the Privy Council. So he knew from his own experience, as well as that of trusted men like Rokeby, precisely how efficient this system could be.

The actions in the Star Chamber were balanced, of course, by two other high courts, Requests and the Chancery. Without their power for mercy, Lambarde might not have shown as much admiration for the Star Chamber as he expressed in this essay. During his early years as a justice, he had evinced some suspicion of it in his Charges to the Jurors, possibly because in those years he was trained as a common lawyer in the handling of evidence and believed in the jury system.

Now came his greatest triumph as the author of *Eirenarcha*. During the Michaelmas Term of 1590, the Queen through her Privy Council ordered that revision be made of the Commission of the Peace. After eleven years of waiting, Lambarde's criticism to Bromley had finally won over delay. The officers charged with this responsibility were Sir Christopher Wray, the Chief Justice of England; Sir Edmund Anderson, the Chief Justice of the Common Pleas; and Sir Roger Manwood, the Chief Baron of the Exchequer. They were joined in this very difficult task by the remainder of the judges and barons of the Coif. And they apparently proceeded with dispatch to make the necessary revisions.

Lambarde then had nineteen passages to revise in his next edition of *Eirenarcha*. As a matter of fact, the edition of 1591 was partially printed when these corrections that he had asked for finally were made by the chief judges of England. Whereupon Lambarde wrote a "forewarning to the readers" of his 1591 edition, concerning this accomplishment: "to purge the late Commission of the Peace from all its imperfections for which this book of mine had long together challenged." Furthermore, he decided that the readers with earlier printings of *Eirenarcha*, as well as any booksellers with stocks of these earlier printings, should benefit. So he listed in this edition the necessary corrections so that readers could strike out the deficient statements and substitute the new provisions. (Subsequent editions, for example, of 1592 and 1594, were reprinted to conform to the new Commission.) And at last his contention was proved correct. This added to his prestige and also to the usefulness of his handbook.

While Lambarde was growing in prestige, he apparently did not appear at the quarter sessions in Maidstone, although he continued to reside at Halling Palace with his children. Doubtless he spent some time in his rooms in Lincoln's Inn during term time, but, strikingly enough, after spending so many years with the elder George Multon, there was no record of continuing visits with the younger George Multon, his first wife's brother. And there evidently was delay in settling the estate of George Multon, for not until February 4, 1591, did Lambarde sign an agreement with his brother-in-law and wife, Audrey, concerning his moiety in the Manor of St. Cleres, Ightham. Although no marriage contract between Lambarde and Jane Multon has come to light, the obviously close association with Jane's father before and after this marriage probably involved Lambarde in Multon's estate, if only in the matter of Jane's dowry. Since George grew up with his sister and Lambarde residing at St. Cleres, Ightham, rather than at Westcombe in East Greenwich, some deep-felt resentment may have long existed in the younger man's heart and mind. Lambarde's companionship with George's father might have seemed like an usurpation of Multon's affection. (Whatever the undisclosed facts were, the negotiation of this settlement was preserved by merest chance on a document bearing Audrey's seal and signature.)

After two years of absence from the quarter sessions, Lambarde returned on September 28, 1591, to give the Charge to the Jurors. The opening seemed composed of paraphrases of certain passages from the first book of *Eirenarcha;* that is, he reemphasized the juror's duty to inquire and present as they had taken oath to do in ancient times, since King Edward III. He elaborated upon the differences between the English and the Roman law:

> The law or policy of this realm of England, as it is a peculiar government, not borrowed of the imperial or Roman law (as be the laws of the most part of other Christian nations) but standing upon the highest reason, selected even for itself; so doth it in one special thing above any other most apparently vary from the usage of other countries: I mean in the manner of proceeding that we have by jurors, which our law calleth the judgment by peers or equals, and that as well in civil questions that do arise privately between man and man as also in criminal causes that lift up the head against the commonwealth, in the latter of which we are not, as other nations, to be accused or indicted at the pleasure or for the gain or malice of any one or a few men but by the oaths and consciences of the twelve at the least, and in either of which we enjoy this singular freedom and prerogative that we are not to be peremptorily sentenced by the mouth of the judge, as other peoples are, but by the oath and verdict of jurors that be our equals, and the same not strangers born but our own countrymen, not far dwelling but of the nearest neighborhood that we have.

Then he gave a forceful description of how the Star Chamber had begun and developed because of the failure of the jurors in ancient times to do their sworn duties:

> For why did one statute erect the Court of Star Chamber and without any use of juries to endow it with an ordinary jurisdiction over riots, retainers, embraceries, and

some other misdem[ean]ors but only upon this reason and pretense: that jurors in their countries either durst not or would not deal faithfully in the discovery of them? Why did another statute provide that a great sort of other offenses should, upon information made for the King, be heard and determined by the only discretion of the justices of peace, without any jury at all but only upon this ground that through the great favor and corruption of inquests they were not punished as by law they ought?

He asked the jurors why Parliament enacted statutes if men like themselves continued to wink at or shut their eyes to evildoers. He spoke very severely, like a father chastising unruly children. He explained the difference between civil and criminal cases and emphasized how necessary it was for them as jurors to see that offenders of the law be punished. He pointed out that if instead of giving relief and alms to rogues, people would not be so foolish if they would report what was going on. Then he declared that these assemblies could accomplish more than even the investigations conducted by twenty Provost Marshals sent into Kent from Westminister.

His impassioned plea was filled with references to customs and procedures, as if he were not merely preparing their minds, as he had often said, but educating them in the process of the law and their part in its enforcement. Thus his attitude appeared now to have changed from that of the local magistrate who had sought the cooperation of the jurors. Now the authority of the learned judge, who had returned home, issued instruction and warning to the jurors that he would tolerate no casual performance of their duties.

One reason for this change in the temper of his Charges might be ascribed to his recent experiences and his intensive study of the high courts of England. He was now revising this manuscript to be known as "Archeion," in which his essay on the Star Chamber formed a major part; this manuscript, of which there were several copies made at this time, was finished at Lincoln's Inn on October 22, 1591. He dedicated it to Robert Cecil, Lord Burghley's son, in recognition of the singular favors of "your father." In looking backward, one can readily understand why Lambarde hesitated to become Burghley's deputy in the Office of Alienations, for he probably had at that time written several of these essays, like that on the Star Chamber, dealing with other high courts, but had not put his work into final form. In this autumn of 1591, he might have shown "Archeion" to Burghley with intention of dedicating this important book to him and at this juncture accepted the suggestion to give it to Robert. For Burghley was using every means at his command to establish his son in his own position of power; he had already given many of the closely guarded records to Robert and thus had made his son essential to the functioning of the government. Dedication of Lambarde's new book to Robert might be of some use in establishing him as the sponsor of this important book about the high courts.

Lambarde probably recognized that Burghley was his chief patron; but if he had followed his heart, he might have dedicated the book to Sir Thomas Egerton. At the moment, however, Robert Cecil could not be denied; Lord Burghley still outranked Egerton, though the Solicitor General's star was rising now with accelerated speed to the zenith of the political firmament.

"Archeion, or, A Discourse Upon the High Courts of Justice in England," dealt with the development of all the high courts of England.[7] Lambarde listed the King's Bench, Court of Star Chamber, Constable's Court, Marshalsea, Admiralty, Gaol Delivery, Oyer and Terminer. This enumeration was both historical and descriptive of the venue by which a case might progress from the local hearing and determination to a high jurisdiction.

His discussion of the Chancery was particularly incisive: "For remedy in which cases of Uses, chiefly the Chancery Court was fled into, as the onely Altar of helpe and refuge: But whensoever this Court of Equity tooke beginning to be a distinct Court, I have made proofe (as I thinke) that the power thereof was always in exercise." He next emphasized "the help of God which speaketh in that Oracle of Equity." He endeavored then to show how the mercy of the sovereign extended through the Chancellor's office to bestow help directly to deserving persons whose causes had become confused in the courts of common law.

He explained that Her Majesty's authority extended over all the courts of law, as God's deputy of justice and equity within the realm. Here was the basis of his thinking of how the three divisions, ecclesiastical, civil, and criminal, had gained absolute authority. He discussed the itinerate justices from the courts of law in Westminister, who from the beginning of the King's Bench, made semiannual visitations to the counties on carefully arranged schedules to conduct the Assizes and Gaol Deliveries. Although Lambarde made clear that there were multiple responsibilities, which appeared to trespass upon the authority of one or more jurisdictions, the unifying principle, undergirding the entire structure of justice from its base to its apex, was the authority of the sovereign. The final determination of any case was in the will of the sovereign, manifested ultimately in the High Courts of Star Chamber, Requests, and the Chancery. He suggested that a man might sue his rights in the base court at home before proceeding outside the county. But if he did not recover his rights in this beginning, he then was able to seek justice in the King's High Court, where not only "right and law" but also "equity and good conscience" prevailed. Then he explained that from ancient sources it was clear that equity was available at the discretion of the sovereign. Thus the hand of the sovereign reached out to relieve the citizen from the rigor of the law; on the other hand, the sovereign with his peers and the "Court of Parliament" created the laws which were to be enforced under the sovereign's authority.

He described the work of the courts of law dealing with civil actions, between the King and his subjects, and he enumerated them: The Court of Exchequer, the Court of Wards and Liveries, the Court of the Duchy of Lancaster, and also Chancery, "at least so farr forth as the same hath to doe with petitions, *travers iuram, de droit,* etc.," and technical instances of *certiorari.* The courts dealing with civil or common pleas were the Admiralty and the King's Bench. The two courts designated as "Courts of Conscience" were the Court of Requests and Chancery.

These technical matters might not be of interest to the general reader beyond the point of recognizing the frequent references to conscience, oaths in the sight of God, and the sovereign as God's deputy, as concepts repeated many times by Lambarde in his Charges to the Jurors. Yet, after all, the ancient origin and continuous development of these courts were significantly different from those of the Roman or European courts. The English law was firmly based on the concept of God's concern for order in both the macrocosm of His universe and the microcosm of England. Moreover, order meant justice, and justice required the punishment of evildoers. On the other hand, equity required the understanding of extenuating circumstances beyond the letter of the law. In Lambarde's final analysis, the law was reason applied to the necessity of maintaining order and peace in the realm.

Although it might seem that by the end of 1591 Lambarde had achieved the height of his productivity and honors, the years of awards to him were just beginning. Life progressed to a fitting climax for this quiet scholar who had given of himself so faithfully to seeking out the enemy within the country. Much of the recognition that "Archeion" might have brought him at this time was not forthcoming, except by the few persons who had procured copies of his manuscript. This unfortunate impasse in Lambarde's reputation resulted from the failure of Robert Cecil to sponsor "Archeion." It remained unprinted. (As a matter of fact, it was not printed until thirty-four years after Lambarde's death, at which time it was recognized by such a perceptive fighter for liberty as the poet John Milton, who copied two sentences from it in his commonplace book and carefully indicated his source.) Probably nothing could have been more discouraging to Lambarde than to have this book lie dormant.

The significance of these legal technicalities, such as the history of the Alienations Office and its accounting, as well as the history of the high courts of England, may on first impression be dismissed. Like any scholarly or technical report coming to the attention of the general reader today, the details of the substance appear to belong to the specialists. But in these instances, both pieces of writing are clear enough for the novice to comprehend if he so wishes, however unprepared he may be to use the material. The point is that though "Archeion" was not printed, copyists did make the manuscript available and it continued to be discussed through the years after Lambarde's death, so that two printings were justified during the crucial period in which the English people were concerned with taking the life of King Charles I.

Editors' attribution of the essay on the Alienations Office to Sir Francis Bacon is high praise indeed for the clarity of its style and recognition of the contribution. Even if Lambarde's reputation might appear to have suffered from Cecil's neglect of the manuscript, it is likely that the right people in the government read copies of the manuscript and thus had opportunity to appraise Lambarde's work. This private esteem did, in fact, become important to him in the following years, even if his public reputation remained enhanced only by his advance to important offices.

Students of legal history seek out the established lines of development in recounting these years in the sixteenth century and have until recently readily dismissed the importance and influence of this book, *Archeion,* printed too long after Lambarde's death to seem to belong to the fifteen-nineties. Lambarde became important as a writer after his death, and his picture appeared on the frontispiece of books, along with engravings of other learned men, in the seventeenth century. Then suddenly all glory ended for him after the restoration of King Charles II. And not until the middle of the twentieth century was he restored partially to his rightful place.

When Lambarde presented his manuscript to Robert Cecil in 1591, the political decline of Queen Elizabeth was beginning. Perhaps as early as 1588, after the glorious defeat of the Armada and the death within the month of the Earl of Leicester, the seeds of the decline were sown. For the Earl had been a symbol to the people, the supporter of the Queen in the public's eye, and his death ended a period of glory. In contrast to the jubilation over the victory, the subsequent years brought gloom and apprehension. Scientists were explaining that the Earth was not the center of the universe as Ptolemy had indicated. The Copernican theory of the sun at the center placed the Earth among the planets revolving around the sun. Theologians were slow to accommodate this concept to their established doctrines. And the people, little understanding either the scientists or the theologians, received only garbled versions of the new order, as poets and essayists began to write with depressed spirits.

In these years of pessimism and misgivings, the harsh facts of paying for the war did not help to raise men's spirits. On the contrary, the new assessments seemed to penalize the rising new class of adventurers and merchant princes, as the old order, symbolized by the Earl of Leicester, passed away. Moreover, the war with Spain, France, and Italy was not won after all. Although the second great Armada did not sail until 1596, faulty communications and fears provided enough rumors to terrify the people. As a consequence of these different causes of unrest in various levels of society, maintenance of law and order became increasingly difficult in the villages as well as in the cities. Cutpurses, who either refused to work or were unable to find jobs, roved the dark streets and country lanes. The alehouses provided release from the humdrum of existence and also stimulated the irresponsibles to plunder and kill.

The church, which might have been a bulwark against disorder, was itself rent with dissention. Various sects of liberal persuasions met in secret as did the Family of Love satirized by Thomas Middleton, one of Shakespeare's contemporaries, in *The Family of Love*. Ben Jonson, who loved Shakespeare "this side of idolatry" wrote comedies "to strip the ragged follies of the time as naked as at their birth."

The golden Elizabethan Age with its monuments of splendor also had its seamy side of bestiality, and in the midst of its vulgarity and brutality loomed the idealistic and forceful figure of Lambarde. He knew from observation what was actually going on. He believed that required churchgoing with attendance taken by the parish officers was not enough. For at the heart of all of his Charges to the Jurors lay the basic idea of conscience before God. For people less dedicated to faith, however, the continuing conflict between Roman Catholics, Anglicans, and various Protestant sects destroyed the authority and serenity of the religious life. In the workaday world of the courts of law, Lambarde was, for all of his knowledge of history, an eminently practical administrator.

Some justices of the peace, like Thomas Harman, the author of *A Caveat for Common Cursetors* (1567), sat smugly in their houses and looked out the window at the wandering rogues and vagabonds passing by on the highway. But while he thus found material for an amusing book about roguery, he himself did nothing to change the conditions. This attitude, in contrast to Lambarde's, was typical of the period. The low classes were stupid, ill-smelling louts, fit to be underpaid laborers and servants loaded down with the dirty work that had to be done. Simply nothing could be done for such people. They were merely objects of derision and contempt. The idea that they might have a home and a garden did not occur to the country squires, or, if it did, they did nothing about it lest they lose some of the retinue of servants required to care for their own establishments.

Bethlehem Hospital in London, known as Bedlam, housed the city's mentally ill, but the "halfwits" in the villages and towns had no asylum from the jeers of local people. Shakespeare's representation of Edgar as disguised as Tom o' Bedlam in *King Lear* had meaning for his audience in the Globe Theatre that cannot be grasped fully by a present-day theater audience. The mentally sick persons rented out from Bedlam to amuse the wedding guests in Middleton's *The Changeling* reflected the ignorance of the time.

The glorification of the Age of Elizabeth by historians and literary scholars has created an idealized picture of the way the rich and talented lived their exciting and interesting lives, as if the so-called poor laws enacted by Parliament in 1570 and 1576 actually had alleviated conditions among the poor. Literary scholars have established neat aesthetic standards for debating justice as derived from Aristotle and Plato, and in particular from the writings of the great church thinkers from St. Augustine to the present. But legal justice appears to be a separate world in which Sir Edward Coke, Sir Francis Bacon, and Sir Thomas Egerton contended brilliantly and learnedly for power.

In the aristocratic view of history, the surging of the people became plots and rebellions against the established order. But there can be no denying the fact that Queen Elizabeth herself recognized that the established order depended upon the central government's reaching out into every field and village with authority. And that authority was vested in the justice of the peace. The trouble was that men like William Gardiner, a notorious justice of the peace, used their authority for private profit. Doubtless there were many like Gardiner. On the other hand, many justices held the feudal view that they, like the great overlords of feudal courts, merely waited until their neighbors, or they themselves, had cause for grievance. They waited to preside and felt no obligation to do more than perhaps attend Parliament and enact another law which might be enforced if conditions were expedient.

Among the justices of the peace, Lambarde was a notable catalyst who was not content with the status quo. Probably there were others like him, but they did not write books that provided the means for standardizing procedures. Lambarde's books set him apart from the other justices, as did his personal efforts in establishing his College for the Poor of Queen Elizabeth, and his leading the Kentish justices to establish a House of Correction. These two establishments were later used as patterns by other men just as interested in human welfare as Lambarde. But it was Lambarde's initiative that paved the way.

Chapter 7

IN THE CHANCERY
AND HUMAN RELATIONS
(1592–1596)

The death of Lord Chancellor Hatton, in 1591, imposed upon the Queen the most difficult task of appointing a successor, as the conflicts among her Privy Councillors old and young were bitter and of serious consequences to the realm. Mindful of her selection of Hatton for reasons other than his knowledge of the law, and unwilling to favor one faction of her contending peers over the other, she chose Sir John Puckering, a respected barrister whose ambitions had not got out of hand.

Among the multifarious duties of the Lord Chancellor, or Lord Keeper of the Great Seal, as Elizabeth designated Puckering, was conducting the proceedings of the High Court of Chancery. This prestigious court, which had represented from earliest times the sovereign's conscience in granting relief from the severity of the judgment rendered in the courts of common law, was truly a court of equity, although the prerogative court of Star Chamber instructed its commissioners to hear and determine cases with "justice and equity." But in Chancery the sovereign's mercy transcended the restrictions on evidence properly admitted to a common law court and accepted testimony, extenuating circumstances, and intercessions to Her Majesty. It was also a court of final review in which the Chancellor or Lord Keeper had the privilege of revealing Her Majesty's will in these matters.

Puckering forthwith appointed Lambarde a Master in the Chancery. This high honor came to Lambarde in recognition of his learning and experience, for Puckering could scarcely afford just to remember an old friend when he required expert judicial minds to assist him in the Chancery amidst all his multifarious duties. Even if Puckering and Lambarde had been called to the bar at Lincoln's Inn twenty-five years earlier on the same day, this appointment would have to be on better grounds than long friendship, for after all, with the Queen's concern with the competency of judges the final approval remained the prerogative of Her Majesty.

Lambarde was a well-known and respected author. In this great upsurge of literary achievement in England during the years immediately following the defeat of the Armada, Shakespeare began writing his plays. The rising pride in being an Englishman almost made England herself the heroine of the chronicle history plays that first made Shakespeare famous. Edmund Spenser was glorifying Elizabeth in *The Faerie Queene:* the conditions of her reign after the twelve moral virtues of Aristotle's devising. And this age had its ideal courtier, scholar, and soldier in Sir Philip Sidney, whose *Arcadia* had set an example for measured prose. His sonnet cycle *Astrophel and Stella* was to rival Spenser's *Amoretti*. And the shocking murder of Christopher Marlowe did not end poetic drama but reminded Englishmen of his achievement and thus obliquely gave impetus to the national drama. In such a dawning respect for learning and writing, the government needed scholars on the bench.

In looking back on Lambarde's appointment, there can be

no doubt that Elizabeth had ample reasons for admiring Lambarde's learning in the law and his ability to write, despite the numerous occasions since he first attended Parliament when his bold independence and integrity annoyed her and tried her patience. She knew well how much Lord Cobham depended upon his loyal service and that Lord Burghley had subsequently made Lambarde his deputy in the Alienations Office. And Rokeby had selected him to serve with him on various commissions. So Lambarde was one of those men whom everyone used.

Nor was there any reason for Elizabeth to forget and eventually to be grateful to him for his ten-year campaign with *Eirenarcha* against the errors in the Commission of the Peace that Bromley had hastily compiled on her order. Lambarde's sharp-eyed devotion to her merited recognition.

Even if *Archeion* remained unprinted, copies of it were written out in commonplace books and the contents of that history of the high courts widely dispersed among important persons; perhaps even the Queen herself had read portions of it. But she could scarcely have avoided hearing of it. So perhaps no man in the legal profession at that time had spent more hours and revealed more perception of the rolls and ancient manuscripts than had Lambarde.

Lambarde probably influenced both Elizabeth and Puckering in trying to raise the standards of the justices of the peace. For at this time, Shakespeare was ridiculing the country justices Shallow and Silence in *King Henry IV, Part II* and pointing out how readily justices allowed a riot to remain a Star Chamber matter rather than settling a disturbance among three or four persons. Indeed Puckering's duties included the Court of Star Chamber, where cases of treason and heresy received summary judgment. This prerogative court, composed of members of the Privy Council, provided quick and final adjudication of hearings and determinations made in cases of alleged offenders against the security of the state. These offenses grouped under the general terms of treason and heresy could involve the most formidable peer or the weakest servant who had plotted to overthrow the government or the state religion.

The Court of Star Chamber reached out to remote hamlets and entered into the finest castles. Sir Francis Walsingham's great network of spies and agents at home as well as abroad provided the material for numerous investigations ranging from witchcraft to money paid to foreign negotiators. No one was secure in those changing times. This court brandished the sword of justice over the heads of justices of the peace, the jurors, and the parish officers who were derelict in their duties, and it established respect for the law.

Since no one knew more than Lambarde about the working system of the Commission of the Peace, his counsel and advice in his new office was available as primary information to Lord Keeper Puckering. At this crucial time in local government, the power of Queen Elizabeth was no stronger than the weakest justice of the peace, and now that Lambarde was in position to review cases in the Chancery, he could point out to Lord Keeper Puckering precise instances of weaknesses in the local government.

Puckering appeared in a dramatic scene in the Court of Star Chamber to demand review of the persons acting as justices of the peace in various counties. He described how Queen Elizabeth took the list of names and indicated from her own knowledge of these men the ones she considered unfit to serve. When she had given back the list of justices, she asked Puckering and the Lord Treasurer to indicate others who in their opinion should be dismissed. So now Puckering was bringing this list to the attention of the Privy Council in order to make a thorough clearance of incompetency. He went on to say that Her Majesty, like a good housewife taking store of her servants, had a personal concern with this problem.

Here again Lambarde's influence may be detected, as he had established the standards for conducting hearings and determinations when justices acted outside and within the quarter sessions. He certainly knew who among the justices in Kent were ignorant or lazy. He could have named these men and aroused concern for the competency of justices in other counties. Then, too, as cases were accumulating in the Chancery, he had found judicial errors that could be traced directly to particular justices. After many years, he had the joy of seeing his work for the improvement of these criminal courts and the magistrates finally brought to a high professional level.

His work in the Chancery required Lambarde to spend more time in London than in Kent, but he continued to return even in these years, twice annually, to deliver at Maidstone his charge to the jurors. A careful comparison of the temper and substance of these last Charges that he uttered reveal striking differences between them and the early ones, those before he became a Master in the Chancery.

While he personally spent many weeks now in term time in his rooms in Lincoln's Inn, he had moved his young family from Halling Palace to his inherited manor of Westcombe in East Greenwich. In Greenwich they were accessible in a short day's ride on horseback, and at his age surely another day would be required to reach Halling. Moreover, he had married a third time. This event took place within two months of his appointment to the judgeship in Chancery.

Five years had passed since Sylvestria's death. His "babes" required more supervision than he could now possibly give, even with a retinue of housekeeper, servants, and nursemaids. His bride was Margaret Reder, who also had been married twice before. But conjectures about his selection of her lead to no conclusions. Ordinarily widows of rich men were in demand, since they brought accumulated wealth for the new husband to expend. Surely Mistress Reder, unlike Sylvestria, brought him no fortune. Lambarde might have fallen in love at fifty-six. What seems likely is that she had served in his household, and to make her legally the stepmother was the easiest procedure for a man with many duties.

Margaret Reder was the daughter of John Payne, a yeoman of Frittenden; her mother was the daughter of Robert Couchman, a clothier. She evidently was very young when she married her first husband, John Meryman, a mason, in Boughton Monchelsey, Kent. The child of this marriage died before baptism. Then, after the death of her husband, she married Richard Reder, the brother of her sister's husband. None of these facts appear unusual, but they would sustain the supposition that she was domesticated, a proper person of simple and unambitious background, the type content to remain at home with the children while her husband spent much of his time in London.

On the day after his marriage on April 3, 1592, Lambarde appeared in Maidstone to give the Charge to the Jurors at the quarter sessions. On this occasion, he uttered an old Charge for the first time in his life, one delivered first on April 16, 1588. Perhaps it was coincidence. Either he married in haste, or the justice assigned to deliver a Charge was unable to do so. Perhaps a courier arrived from Lord Cobham to request Lambarde's service, whereupon Lambarde looked over his file for a suitable Charge. It would normally be one previously delivered in the springtime, the most important of the quarter sessions. So the bridegroom hastily departed on horseback for Maidstone, and later changed the date on his manuscript.

This Charge was one of the most severe that he had ever given, and strangely enough it was still appropriate. When he had written it in 1588, England was waiting for the Armada, but now four years after the victory, England was again expecting invasion from either across the Channel or another Armada, which it was rumored was ready to sail.

He declared that recusants, Jesuit priests, and witches continued to agitate the people and that such actions were evil. The people themselves were indulging in excessive drinking and unlawful games of chance; indeed, instead of working, they were content "to gad about" in their bright clothes and loiter. After all, he had found that human nature had not changed in the four years since he had first written this exhortation. Yet, as a matter of fact, social conditions were continuingly changing. Merchants were making more money than before because the people were spending their money on various items not available to them during the hard times just before and after the coming of the Armada. If now their country was to be threatened again with invasion, they would at least spend this interval between wars in pleasurable living. Lambarde had no understanding of such irresponsibility, for his work had become his life. So he thundered away at the jurors, using his ponderously sonorous sentences as if he were in the pulpit instead of on the bench.

Now he did a characteristic thing as a Master in the Chancery. As upon his appointment to the Commission of the Peace he had prepared a guide which became *Eirenarcha,* and as when he served in the Alienations Office he wrote a history and gave an accounting of the office, now he began to collect cases from the Chancery Rolls. He had the common lawyer's curiosity about precedents and unusual findings in this high court, though he had already included a history of this court in *Archeion.* His present concern was the compilation of a casebook. (Historically minded lawyers know this book well as *Cary's Reports,* printed in 1650; the full title reads: *Reports on Causes in Chancery, Collected by Sir*

*George Carye, one of the Masters of the Chancery, in Anno
1601; out of the Labours of Mr. William Lambert.*)

In Elizabethan London books separated the gentlemen
scholars from the roistering gallants who also frequented the
walks around St. Paul's Cathedral. In the shops across the
streets surrounding this great church were the printers' establishments, with their ornamented signs, such as the Pied Bull,
where one of the most interesting quartos of Shakespeare's
King Lear was printed and sold.

Lambarde had one of the finest libraries, though by no
means the largest. Its quality was evidenced in the rare
books that he possessed, the fine typesetting on rich paper,
the fine leather and vellum bindings. But he was a difficult
man to whom a book could be given, for he showed no interest
in the current outpouring of poems, plays, and essays. His
taste was revealed in collecting books of law from the finest
printers in Europe, classical studies of history and in particular
agriculture. He took delight in these practical matters of
how people had actually lived, rather than in the fiction of
the creative imagination.

His old friend William Sedley gave him a beautiful book
dealing with the law, entitled *Vocabularium iuris utrivsque*
(London, 1586). Lambarde apparently thought so much of
this gift that he inscribed it with his signature in Latin and
wrote "didi Quilielo Sedley, 1592." This was the kind of
book that Lambarde prized, though, because it was a legal
scholar's book, very few of his contemporaries would have
read it.

At this time the plague was raging in London, and there
was a scarcity of bread because of the poor growing conditions
for the grain the preceding spring and summer. These conditions were so serious that the Queen called Parliament into
session on January 14, 1592, to provide some relief. Three
days later Lambarde addressed a special commission which

he addressed as "You gentry, and the rest, that be sworn," rather than his customary "neighbors and friends" used in his Charges to Jurymen. So it is evident that the seriousness of this situation required a special kind of jury for this inquiry.

Her Majesty's Special Commission was read aloud to the assembly before Lambarde began his address in which he reiterated the four principal issues to be considered: first, Her Majesty's provisions, "charitably made," have been diverted from relief of the poor to private profit; second, this abuse of Her Majesty's purpose must be speedily corrected; third, Her Majesty has placed special trust in us as her commissioners; and last, she has given us the authority and directions to carry out this service.

The interesting feature of this Charge to the Jurors, the thought that separates it from all other Charges, was its practicality. It gave the impression that Lambarde had been doing some original thinking about the problem in Kent. Heretofore he had advocated the whipping and branding of beggars who loitered along the great highways in Kent, and even now he declared that these homeless men were committing all kinds of "mischief," which he particularized as pilfering, drunkenness, lechery, bastardy, and murder. But this time he insisted that these swarms of beggars must be kept under surveillance and given work to do, as much as their bodies would bear. They must be taught how to work for the country's good.

This was the first time that he recognized responsibility for these homeless creatures who wandered aimlessly after leaving a ship in a Kentish port or being detached from a regiment. He pointed out that unless these unfortunates worked, they would starve, "or all of us in the commonwealth would have to supply at our own expense the food which now they took from others." He then referred to Lazarus and the crumbs denied from the table. But this concept would apply only to the poor for whom he himself had shown pity and given sustenance. So he had the dilemma of advocating food for those persons who refused to work, and for whom he had no pity, as he had ordered them to be whipped and branded. This concept of responsibility seemed to evolve from necessity, as if he and the commissioners had to accept the problems arising from new conditions.

Of great social significance was his pointing out in this Charge that the number of the poor had increased; indeed, the conditions of war had created a new kind of poor. Upon inquiry, he had found a dearth of things "needful for life," food, clothing, and places to live and work. He recognized, for example, the increase in the rents of the land possessed by both the church and the state.

And to the increase of these eveils, we have, as I said, a sort of poor lately crept in amongst us and not before known to our elders: I mean poor soldiers, of whom this commission specially speaketh. There were always poor leprous, poor lazarous, aged poor, sick poor, poor widows, poor orphans, and suchlike, but poor soldiers were either rarely or never heard of till now of late. . . . Nevertheless we are by many duties most bounden to help and relieve them, considering that they fight for the truth of God and defense of their country; yea, they fight our own war and do serve in our places, enduring cold and hunger when we live at ease and fare well, lying in the open field when we are lodged in our beds of down, and meeting with broken heads and limbs when we find it good and safe sleeping in a whole skin.

This impassioned and perceptive Charge revealed that Lambarde could think precisely to the point. He closed this long speech with the admonition to please God by unmasking robbers for the good of the country. Perhaps the presence of the gentry stimulated him as much as the cause. Whatever the reason, he transcended his usual preparation of the jurors' minds. With added authority as a Master in the Chancery, he was not content with uttering a competent Charge, and he apparently had raised his standard beyond his usual explanation of ancient customs, the reasonableness of the law, and obligations of the jurors. He quoted and translated Latin phrases to illustrate his ideas; he used the metaphor of the law as medicine not received in the body if "shut up in books." He was precise in referring to the "grand jurymen" as the primary persons in the Commission, without whose search and inquiry there would be no information by which evildoers could be tried and punished.

He also pointed out that the "grand jurymen" were not to make decisions of what to report or omit as if they were "justices of *nisi prius* and of gaole delivery." They were to report all offenders, without deciding not to report some of them; but with single purpose to inquire and present, they would present offenders of the law for judgment at this time and in this place.

As new threats of invasion were reported from sources on the Continent, and the lack of bread became an acute problem, Her Majesty appeared dissatisfied with the slowness of the Kentish commissioners to comply with the composition of grain for her own household and stable. But conditions were complex at this time, and the composition for the marshes of Romney, for example, had led to requests for moderation of the imposed assessment of purveyance. These people had maintained the beacons along the coast, the harboring of the Royal Navy, preparations of castles and blockhouses, and they had given these services very often without any recompense.

Conditions were further complicated for these people of

Romney because adjacent ecclesiastical properties, belonging to both the dioceses of Canterbury and Rochester, limited their resources. Such income as they derived from grasses, salt, and certain fish had already been used in Her Majesty's service before they were required to meet this order for composition.

Such were the findings that Lord Cobham presented to Queen Elizabeth, as a result of inquiry made by Lambarde's two close friends, Sir William Fludd and Sir William Sedley. An ironic aspect of this social problem was that the gentry were seeking means of relieving the poor, while they themselves were paying out large parts of their incomes in these assessments made by the Crown. Yet, as everyone knew, the great peers with their monopolies were often in debt and borrowing from Queen Elizabeth. In retrospect Lambarde appeared to be in a better position as one of the gentry than as a knight insofar as assessments were concerned; and half of his lands were involved in the endowment of his College for the Poor.

During this period of being a Master in the Chancery, Lambarde apparently received many letters and preserved some of them for posterity.[1] Many of these unprinted letters deal with pleas to Lambarde as a Master in the Chancery. In the twentieth century, direct appeals from litigants to the judge about a case pending in a high court might raise more than an eyebrow; but in the sixteenth century, such procedure was customary and usually embellished with gifts. Quite apart from the experience of Lambarde, but an example of an honorable man, was the appeal of Alexander Nowell, the redoubtable Dean of St. Paul's Cathedral, to no less a person than Sir Thomas Egerton, then Solicitor General. This letter is dated July 7, 1590, and includes the sentence: "I shall be much bounden unto your worship, unto whom I send a poor token, for the antiquity rather than for the value of the same." Both of these gentlemen were of the highest integrity; the letter evidenced only standard procedure, but it would indicate much about Lambarde's thinking.

Sir Richard Lewkner, for example, wrote to Lambarde on February 8, 1594 (an unpublished letter), about Edmund Fairmanner. After the death of his father, Edmund Fairmanner "sued his livery" and also "sued a pardon of alienation upon the purchase," and now he had been called into the Chancery on some new premise that Lawkner did not understand, presumably the dower of his mother, to whom Lambarde had apparently paid £4 in rent out of the court in lieu of dower. So Lewkner requested justice, as the young man was poor.

Although Lewkner resided in the Middle Temple, his letter is written in odd script, without punctuation and with evident predilection for rare words. He had no doubt whatsoever about how this case should properly be handled, and frankly asked for favor. That Lewkner was a testy and unpleasant man at times is clear from another unprinted letter addressed to the Privy Council (May 8, 1601) after he had examined the various ways in which the deputy lord lieutenants had expended money for outfitting soldiers pressed into Her Majesty's service from various counties. (The same eccentricities of script and expression occur here as in the letter to Lambarde.) He was a hard man, but the Queen appointed him to be Chief Justice in the counties palatine of Chester and Flint, and justice in the counties of Denbigh and Montgomery, as she informed the Lord President of the Council of Wales. As a matter of fact, another unprinted manuscript deals with the assignment of Lewkner by the Privy Council to investigate the "manner of pay and weekly impresses to her majesties forces" in the lowlands.

Lambarde preserved another letter (unprinted) received a few months later, on July 20, 1594, from George Brooke, the younger son of Lord Cobham. Of course Lambarde could not foresee that nine years later this scholar would lose his head for high treason, but at the moment the fact that young Brooke trusted him with the safekeeping of the deed to his property, the rectory on the Island of Greane, indicated Brooke's confidence in Lambarde's integrity; in fact this letter was a record by which the deed could be located.

Women as well as men wrote to Lambarde concerning cases pending in the Chancery. For example, Anne Peckham wrote to him about her husband's suit against his brother in 1595. (The only readily discernible part of this script was her signature, spelled out in bold letters.) In that year, 1595, controversy had arisen over the family manor of Denham, which had passed to the Crown because of debt. Since, according to the local records, the Peckhams were either Papists or recusant sympathizers, they were now in serious trouble. And through Lambarde was a Protestant, he had not allowed his religious convictions to come between him and justice for the Peckhams.

Sir Francis Walsingham at this time had recognized one way to deal with such problems. He suggested that recusants be permitted to cross the seas and be given aid to establish their lives in the New World. So, on petition of Sir Philip Sidney, Sir George Peckham, and Sir John Gilbert, a special commission had been granted to them for the development of a tract of land in America, an estimated 30,000 acres, some nine years before this present controversy. Now Anne Peckham was evidently the wife of the younger son of this adventurer, Sir George Peckham; the older son bore his father's name; hence her husband was Edmund. As neither she nor Lambarde used the title "Lady," she was simply "Mrs. Peckham," as Lambarde endorsed the letter for his file.

Aside from these sidelights on the family, the letter is interesting because it reveals much of the veneration in which

Lambarde was held. Mrs. Peckham began by acknowledging the "many ways bound unto you," for "fatherly care towards me and mine. My husband has let me understand of your friendly motion for staying of the unnatural suit between him and his brother." She asked Lambarde to continue this stay of the case because further action would be costly to both brothers, and her husband had not engaged in a lawsuit before this.

Poor growing conditions continued and brought "renewed orders for the stay of corn" at a meeting in Stroode Church on December 18, 1594, at which Lambarde addressed the jurors. He began this Charge to "neighbors and friends" with the observation that one of the burdens of princes and those at the "helm of government" was to protect the realm from foreign invasion; in addition it was necessary to give orders if people were to live peacefully together and "plenteously provided of all things that are needful for the maintenance of a good and happy life."

Such a hope, however devoutly it was wished, Lambarde surely knew could not be attained by everyone in this life; it was, of course, the Utopian dream, the escape to the golden age of Arcady, far removed from the present situation of people beset by hunger; nevertheless, he continued for several sentences to glorify the relation of God to the sovereign and the good laws of England. Doubtless he meant it, but he himself had lost the common touch with the people and the realities of their existence.

Finally he came to the thirteen articles by which the jurymen were to seek out those persons who were interfering with the normal flow of grain to market and the distribution of flour for bread. He reminded them that about eight years ago Her Majesty had recognized that "covetous and gready means" would eventually bring a great dearth. Whereupon she graciously had given orders "for the stay thereof" so that the markets were served and the poor people were "fed at home for reasonable monies." So now again, seeing that the kingdom was afflicted, she had commanded the citizens of London to provide great quantities of grain from beyond the sea and therefore had renewed the orders whereof so much good had ensued before.

On the human side, Lambarde's purpose was obviously twofold: he had to allay the peoples' fears which were verging on panic, and he did so with this show of confidence and the reminder that this method had worked before. His second objective was to arouse the jurors to perform the unpleasant and arduous task of canvassing their neighborhoods, asking questions, and looking into granaries in search of hoarded grain. In contrast to official documents and tables of statistics of what happened in December of 1594, this incident revealed disturbed people listening to a notable judge as he tried to quiet their fears and make acceptable a very difficult order handed down from the Crown and the Privy Council. In this crisis the justices were the means, between government and people, for securing the public welfare. This was also an interesting sidelight on Lambarde's career as he returned from his duties in the Chancery to conduct this assembly at Stroode Church—his acceptance of one more responsibility on top of the stack of burdens he was carrying. If other Masters in the Chancery were dispatched to their counties, legal historians need not search for reasons why the cases in Chancery were dammed up so that years often passed before equity could be meted out.

Lambarde interrupted his work in the Chancery to return to Maidstone to deliver the Charge to the Jurors on April 29, 1595. Although this spring meeting of the quarter sessions was, of course, the most important assembly of the year, with the fixing of wages and announcement of various levies and royal compositions, the growing season was again poor and shortage of grains could be expected. But in retrospect Lambarde's leaving his exacting work in the Chancery to prepare this address and travel to Maidstone seems to have been a waste of his energy. He was still a justice of the peace in Kent, to be sure, even while in the Chancery. Possibly this assignment was an honor, or more likely it was desirable to have a person of authority presiding. Whatever the reason, there can be no doubt that Lambarde himself took this task seriously, for he carefully prepared an address more suitable as a model for the young men in Lincoln's Inn to emulate than for the hardhanded jurors to understand.

This was the longest and perhaps the most learned disquisition that he ever uttered on these occasions. It was not only less hortatory and more expository, in preparing the jurors' minds for their duties, but it was also literary. Even though Lambarde was always precise in his use of phrases, he appeared in this Charge to be constructing his sentences as if he were very conscious of how his style of expression would appear to a reader, rather than for its direct impact upon listeners.

"The mark and end of all good laws," he began, "was to charish virtue and to chastise vice, not only in the mind through discourse of inward reason and concepts but also by continual practice. As medicine was required by the natural body of man to purge and cast out evil humors, so in the body politic, laws were the curative medicine against evildoers. Without law to provide security of persons and possessions, force, deceit, corruption, idleness, intemperance, and many other abuses would create a living death. But unless used, medicine cannot aid the body, nor weapons prevail in war; so with these laws, however politically devised, unless carefully and continually used, justice, power, and virtue cannot be drawn from them."

This Charge required the concentrated attention of the

jurors because of its rhetorical embellishments which soared beyond the experience of the farmers, shopkeepers, and other men of good repute who had but little learning in the law. They doubtless thought that he was saying what he should say, and they came away with words and phrases rather than the substance of this learned discourse. Hence the suggestion that Lambarde, knowing the limitations of most of the jurors' minds, wrote with high purpose, as usual, setting forth the principles which students of the law might well consider in addressing jurors. At least he did not "talk down" to his auditors. He stretched their wits to the snapping point.

For several paragraphs Lambarde developed the concept that "we ourselves hold in our hands" the power to gain information by search and inquiry, then to determine by hearing, and finally in this way to execute justice for the good of all. He had uttered these phrases many times before. But now he explained that men under oath committed a serious fault when they obstructed the proceedings by refusing to present information. Lambarde placed the blame squarely upon the jurors as causing the basic fault in the execution of justice, for "without search and inquiry offenses against the law could not be discovered." As the inquirers, seers, and searchers, he said, they were required by the oaths and articles of their charge to bring information from credible witnesses as well as from their own observations. Their fault in not doing so appeared not only in these sessions but also when visiting justices came here for jail delivery and other purposes; even in "trial for life," the jurors failed to heed the evidence. They appeared to have established themselves as justices to determine causes before presenting them, whether alleged offenders were guilty or not.

The remedy of all these faults would therefore be found in the jurors themselves; their responsibility was to inquire and present, he repeated, not to judge. Even the justices could extend this mercy to offenders, except that benefit belonging to the clergy. The prerogative to make free and gracious pardon belonged to Her Majesty; hence it was the duty of the justices at these sessions to report offending jurors, either to the Lords of the Star Chamber or to other jurymen, to levy fines and proceed with punishments.

This threat to report the jurors who failed in their duties was, however, no more than that faced by the justices themselves. On the basis of the revised Commission, Lambarde was no longer seeking cooperation from neighbors and friends but demanding it. His earlier appeals to the jurors were predicated upon local pride, to keep Kent peaceful and secure. Now the interesting feature was that changing conditions had brought many strangers into the county from outside. Provincial standards, the local autonomy, the belief that Kentish men could settle their differences among themselves, now had to be abandoned. Although he had always referred to the authority of the sovereign in his Charges, he had tried to win the jurors by reasoning rather than authority. It is quite possible that his earlier approach to the jurors, stressing responsibility for local conditions, had succeeded, since he was assigned the task of addressing them at least twice a year. Although his emotional appeals had earlier touched the consciences of the jurors, causing them to speak up when they might have remained silent, now he recognized that the changing social conditions had produced new problems which required stern authority. His own view had doubtless widened since his return to London for term time. He had reviewed many cases which should have been equitably settled in the quarter sessions if the justices of the peace had known the law. So he might have been addressing himself as much to his fellows on the bench as to the jurors. Actually, he was performing a service.

Lambarde's assistance of Lord Cobham was suddenly increased when Queen Elizabeth appointed Cobham to be Lord Chamberlain, on the death of her uncle, Lord Hunsdon, who had directed the affairs of this important office for many years with great distinction. Hunsdon had assisted authors and players in the struggle against the Puritan government of London. The Puritans blamed all evil upon the players, not only for immorality in their fiction but also for augmenting the plague by bringing people together in close quarters. The theatrical companies had not been allowed within the precincts of the City. Earlier theaters had been built north of the old Roman Wall and across the River Thames on the bankside. Until his death Hunsdon had proved himself a patron of the arts and a doughty champion for the emerging national drama.

Lord Cobham also fancied himself a patron of the arts, for he had given assistance to writers and acquired manuscripts, books, and art objects. His chief artistic interest was manifest in his building and refinement of Cobham Hall, originally in the form of an E, to which he had added large wings maintaining the balance and symmetry of the structure. He showed taste in selecting designs for ceilings, windows, and archways, and he used imported marble and stone. Such matters, usually left to architects and builders, fascinated him.

Lord Cobham's appointment to the office of Lord Chamberlain came when he was tired and sick. He was worried about the illness of his daughter, who had married Robert Cecil, and he was concerned about his own health. So he called upon Lambarde, Sir John Leveson, and Sir Thomas Fane to prepare his will.

Since Lambarde had gone to the Chancery, Cobham had relied upon Fane and Leveson for assistance with Kentish affairs formerly delegated to Lambarde. But though all three men were to be co-administrators, Lambarde had the responsibility of writing Cobham's will. The value of this estate, comprising many manors, exquisite jewels, and houses, could be appraised in present-day terms as more than two million dollars. Cobham stipulated the building and endowing of an almshouse after the manner of Lambarde's, provision for all of his children, and various benefactions, but the great Lord Burghley and his son, Secretary Cecil, were merely to oversee the settlements. In the midst of these considerations, very delicate for Lambarde's interests, Lord Cobham's daughter died and thus these provisions became complicated with respect to Secretary Cecil.

Cobham's short time in the office of Lord Chamberlain would make difficult any appraisal of his contribution by comparison with the achievement of his predecessor, Lord Hunsdon, or even in contrast to Hunsdon's methods. Yet the most notable incident that took place during his service was entirely personal—Cobham found that Shakespeare had named the chief comic figure in *King Henry IV, Part I* Sir John Oldcastle. Even if it was Shakespeare's intent for his audience to laugh with the witty Oldcastle as much as to laugh at him, the characteristics of this old knight of the castle were broad in scope and vulgar. Sir John as an old man had all the desires of a wild young man without performance except in drinking sack and eating capons. Cobham was outraged because the prototype, the historical John Oldcastle, was his own ancestor. The original Sir John Oldcastle had married the heiress of the third Lord Cobham and thus was six generations removed from the new Lord Chamberlain.

The historical Sir John was a follower of the religious reformer John Wycliffe, as well as the companion of Prince Hal. Oldcastle became Lord Cobham by marriage and was tried for heresy, as a Lollard, and convicted. But he extricated himself from the Tower of London and gained his freedom only to be recaptured and burned as a heretic. Such was the martyr that Cobham found depicted as a drunkard, glutton, lecherer, and colossal liar, the wittiest of men, in Shakespeare's play. But in Lord Cobham's agitated mind whirled many problems real and imagined with which Lambarde had to work.

Another of Lambarde's responsibilities was at Lincoln's Inn in London, apparently on a committee to buy adjacent land and erect a new building. Robert Adams, in an unprinted letter of July 3, 1595, referred to this matter, while writing to Lambarde to inquire if it would be necessary for him to appear in the closing of a case in the Chancery. Robert Adams had gained a reputation as a surveyor in preparation of the earthen works along the coast to defend vantage points against invasion. Now he reported that he was on the Queen's business in Sussex and might possibly come to Kent later to see Lambarde. But he did not want to attend the court to recover the property in the lawsuit that he had won in the Chancery; perhaps he had a sense of humor, for the excuse that he gave was his "lameness."

In looking back on these initial years in the Chancery, Lambarde appeared to be involved in many duties and enterprises apart from his work in the court. As a learned judge to whom many technical details were referred, he seemed to be spending much of his time doing work that could be accomplished by any competent common lawyer. All of these endeavors substantiate earlier appraisals of this man as a person whose life was well ordered and dedicated to hard work.

Chapter 8

THE CLOSING YEARS (1596–1601)

The closing years of Lambarde's life were filled with varied activities in addition to his routine work. For if some of his younger associates referred to him as "old Lambarde," age had not diminished his capacity for hard and exacting work. Though twenty years had passed since the publication of his *A Perambulation of Kent*, the printers were asking him for a revised edition. Moreover, the success of William Camden's *Britannia*, and the establishment of the Society of Antiquarians, had renewed interest in his pioneer work as much perhaps as the changing social conditions which had brought new families to Kent. This edition required few corrections of facts and there were not many additions. Yet one personal reference seems important as an indication that despite his removal to his own manor of Westcombe in East Greenwich, he occasionally visited Halling Palace for a brief sojourn. His love of this place, heretofore expressed in the phrase "my halcyon days," now is fully stated: "At this place of the Bishop of Halling, I am drawing on the last Scaene of my life where God hath given me *Liberorum Quadrigam*, all the fruite that ever I had."

This reference to the "four-horse chariot of freedoms" suggests that here in Halling Palace he enjoyed the first feelings of accomplishment, the purposeful surging forward of his life. For however mystical may seem the attachment of a man of achievement to some particular house, such associations have become almost commonplace. In this place, his children were born in love and it was here that he experienced the sudden sorrow of Sylvestria's death. Nevertheless, at Halling he gained his intimate association with Cobham and Burghley and found the satisfaction of his spirit. For this man of integrity and independence had a deep strain of sentiment, too. So in the 1596 edition of *A Perambulation of Kent* he recorded how he felt about Halling Palace.

Lambarde lost two of his greatest friends in the spring of 1596, Lord Cobham and Ralph Rokeby. Cobham died on March 6 and the will was sealed five days later and proved on May 23, 1596. But nine days after Cobham's death, it was Lambarde's duty to write to Lord Burghley and explain the circumstances undergirding the will, even though a copy of this document had gone posthaste to Lord Burghley and his son, Secretary Cecil. Lambarde had to explain the "secret confidence" that Cobham had placed in him, Leveson, and Fane and the "oversight" of the entire proceedings delegated to Lord Burghley and Secretary Cecil. He stated that £5,600 was provided for the founding of Cobham College, and also furniture for it appraised at 2,000 marks. Other benefactions included £2,000 to relieve the debt of William, the second son; and income for life to George, the third son. These amounts were to be procured from the sale of a dwelling house. Then there was consideration for the poor estate of the children of Cobham's daughter by marriage to Mr. Edward Becher. Finally the distribution of furniture was to be made among the three sons.

Lambarde devoted an entire paragraph of this letter to emphasizing the harmony existing among the three sons. He wrote that he himself had urged Cobham to designate the three brothers to execute their father's will, but Cobham had insisted upon following his own father's precedent of ordaining lawyers to settle his estate. Hence the designation of Lambarde, Leveson, and Fane to be the executors was contrary to Lambarde's advice.

Lambarde's position was particularly delicate since a large sum of money was to be spent on Cobham College, an almshouse to be established and operated in accord with Lambarde's own principles. Certainly here was an example of Lambarde's influence on Cobham, however inactive Lambarde might have been in this matter during the writing of the will. Lambarde had apparently won Cobham's admiration for building and endowing a College for the Poor and Cobham wished to do likewise. The intended honor was embarrassing for Lambarde.

Yet there was little that Lambarde could write to ameliorate the slight to Robert Cecil, who had married Cobham's daughter and might be expected to be an executor of this will. And Lambarde's manuscript of "Archeion" lay in Cecil's possession, unrecognized and unprinted, though dedicated to him.

Lambarde and Leveson proceeded with the establishment of Cobham College in the village of Cobham, using freedom in their interpretation of the testator's wishes. They purchased a farm from George Byng of Wrotham, paying him £300. The farm was located in Shorne, apparently to be a source of income for the endowment of the almshouse. The two trustees further liberalized the regulations for entrance to Cobham College to meet the needs of the time. Cobham's will specified that his College should follow the regulations governing Lambarde's almshouse. But Lambarde's stringent examination of the applicants' religious convictions were now set aside to give relief to poor persons in severe need. According to the records in the parish church at Shorne, the trustees of Cobham College faced the problems and accommodated the rules to the situation.[1] So as Lambarde became president of this new establishment, he appeared flexible in his administration of the rules and principles which he himself had stated for his own institution. (As a matter of record, the trustees fulfilled Cobham's stipulations within a period of two and a half years.)

Despite Cobham's death and the subsequent responsibilities confronting Lambarde, he found time a few weeks later, on April 20, 1596, to address the jurors at the quarter sessions held in Maidstone. This was the important spring assembly at which wages for the year were determined as well as the hearing and determining of presentments, including the alleged culprits bound over during the winter months. So the work of this spring meeting of the local court was invariably heavy and this year it was complicated by poor grain-growing weather. Lambarde knew from experience that there would be a scarcity of grain and so did the farmers among the jurors.

He began by pointing out that in his opinion these assemblies were not held often enough and the time allotted was insufficient for dealing with all the issues. Nevertheless, the slow progress toward the benefits of civil justice could be observed in that the persons here present had not been murdered, nor injured by thieves and vexed by barraters. On the other hand, people seemed to attend these assemblies for the show rather than for justice. But what a happy state of affairs would result if the jurors were alert and willing to perform their duties. And what incredible love would then follow among men.

Lambarde was still trying to set before the jurors the idealism that permeated the theory of the law, even though the jurors did not practice the theory. He illustrated his theory:

· 163 ·

The law may not unaply be resembled to an artificial organ or instrument of music which is prepared with tuneable pipes of all sorts and proportions and which by the help of the bellows and the hand of the organist or player will yield most pleasing and delightful harmony. For the Parliaments, being the common council of the realm, have from time to time devised laws most fit and tuneable for all the degrees of persons living under the obedience thereof, and those also are inspired and blown with the assenting authority of the prince, who desireth nothing more than to satisfy her people with the sweet sounds and strokes of her royal justice. . . . And therefore, seeing that the distribution of our country laws is in great favor put into the hands of you and us, our parts and duty it is so to order and move the same that they may sound out and speak to all, . . .

Once more he was asserting the principle that the law had to be the responsibility of the people. These trials by jury in which they were presently to be engaged depended upon the presentment of complaints. But already many of the jurors had prejudged alleged culprits and consequently had come without presentments to be tried here. Some jurors were afraid to bring complaints against the powerful persons in their communities, others lacked conscience to present their neighbors and friends, and still others sought revenge upon offenders for personal reasons.

Lambarde was thus recognizing the essential weakness of this system. For the jurors came from various districts in Kent to the quarter sessions in Maidstone. But after the assembly was over and they returned home, they had to live with their neighbors. Furthermore, there was no independent constabulary to protect them from revenge. The parish constables and the watch, as Shakespeare revealed in *Much Ado*

About Nothing, were inefficient guardians of the peace. Dogberry, Vergus, and the watchmen, with due allowance for
the exaggeration of satire, were tired from the day's work
and serving the community without remuneration. Even if
the penalties were severe for justices of the peace, jurors, and
parish officers who failed in their duties, the villagers and
the local squires continued to determine their own cases. As
a matter of fact, the justices either alone or in pairs held a
hearing and determined the majority of the misdemeanors;
and if the felon were bound over to the next quarter sessions,
often enough, according to the records, determination of his
case by trial of jury was duly made.

Shortly after the Easter quarter sessions, Ralph Rokeby
died. His last will and testament designated Lambarde and
Sir Thomas Egerton, the Lord Keeper of the Great Seal, to
be co-administrators of his large estate, which was complicated
with bequests to numerous relatives, friends, servants, and
the inmates of hospitals and prisons. And again the burden
of this detailed work fell squarely on Lambarde's shoulders.
Surely the Lord Keeper could not be bothered with such
details, though Egerton has been credited with receiving no
less than £10,000 as an executor's fee.

The distribution of this rich bachelor's estate reveals certain aspects of social responsibility in Elizabethan life, as well
as indicating Lambarde's work on his close friend's benevo-
lences. Lambarde recorded that on July 15, 1596, he had
received the sum of £1970 6s. 2d. He had distributed of this
amount £249 17s. 8d. for the expense of Rokeby's funeral, the
probate of the will, and sundry items which ranged in
amounts from £167 9s. to £167 5s. He listed legacies paid to
fifteen persons for a total expenditure of £285 11s. 3d. He
paid out £33 10s. to Rokeby's five servants for wages and
rewards. A sum in amount of £240 6s. 8d. was paid by Lambarde in bequests to nine kinfolk. Rokeby left £100 for the

endowment of the College for the Poor established by Lambarde. Three persons received a total of £14 4s. 10d. for debts. The prisoners in three jails received a total of £300. The remainder was paid for one outstanding debt and to prisoners in various jails. Lambarde had left £1 2s. 10d. on June 15, 1600, when the final accounting, nearly four years later, was at last made.[2] Of course Lambarde had to depend upon couriers on horseback to reach distant kinsfolk and friends, but his own efficiency in handling the funds had made possible the carrying out of Rokeby's provision within approximately one year, despite the delay in the closing of the estate. Yet it was significant that Lambarde in middle age had given away to his College for the Poor almost as much as Rokeby's final disbursement.

Meanwhile Lambarde's friends intruded for his advice and counsel, as indicated in an unprinted letter from his old friend William Sedley, concerning a lawsuit involving his mother-in-law, a privileged lady of great wealth, and an astute lawyer with whom Sedley had just talked in London. The letter concludes with this tribute to Lambarde's learning and skill: "Whatever you think fit to be done by me you shall find me ready to join you in it, be it so much a continuing problem down to doomsday, if you shall so appoint it."

Amidst all these claims upon his attention, Lambarde was continuing his duties as a Master in the Chancery, a heavy burden since this court was notoriously late in attending to the cases for its review.

Riots broke out in Kent in July, 1596. Carts of grain were overturned and the grain carried away. These rioters were not merely ill-intentioned; they were hungry. The scarcity of grain that Lambarde had anticipated in the spring was now at harvest time fulfilled, and since growing conditions that spring of 1596 were poor all over England, such outbursts occurred not only in Kent but were sufficiently widespread that Elizabeth and her Privy Council had to meet this issue. They sent out orders to all the justices of the peace in various counties to curb these disturbances and to give drastic penalties to offenders. The Queen and her Councillors could not change the weather, but they could send the long-suffering and overburdened justices out to investigate the bins on individual farms and to identify the purchasers of grain. Lambarde had been through this many times before and knew, as a country man, that hungry people must be cared for. The severe winter had thinned out the autumn plantings, and the wet spring had rotted the new plantings as the seeds stood in pools of water. Such conditions stimulated the forestallers, engrossers, and regraters—all the types of withholders of grain from the marketplaces—as in the past to buy up grain at high prices from the farmers. The immediate profit of the farmers and the need for keeping seed for future plantings made the local situations very difficult to determine.

Somehow Lambarde found time to write a Charge to the Jurors at the quarter sessions held in Maidstone on September 28, 1596. This eloquent statement was more thoughtful in presenting the basic philosophy underlying the English common law than was required "to inspire the minds of the jurors." It was less hortatory and more informative than his early Charges to the Jurors, revealing how he himself had advanced in his thinking. It was indeed the kind of sophisticated address more suitable for a Reader's Dinner at Lincoln's Inn, or to be printed as a guide to young law students, than for the farmers who comprised the majority of the jury.

He began simply enough with an explanation of the natural law—how all created things existed within an orderly universe. Then he pointed out that amidst this natural order there did occur tempests, and such disorders accounted for the scarcity of grain. These natural disorders required that administration be made of these discords among people.

"Why do men, who have been terrified by war and rent apart by dissention, fail to maintain order so necessary to their lives?"

Much of the present dissention among Englishmen, he declared, came from foreigners. The French aroused interest in garish and light apparel. (As a matter of fact, at just this time the French were developing new modes of costume.) He described the Dutch as drunkards, the Irish idle, the Scotsmen as quarrelsome, and the Spaniards as sensual and blasphemous. But, he said, the English excelled their teachers in all these vices. Lambarde was thus recording the effect of the war in the lowlands and the travel of English merchants to foreign countries. The changing social conditions brought disturbance to the old order that he had faithfully described in his books.

Then he took up the basic reasons for this assembly. The shortage of grain was caused by engrossers, forestallers, and regraters. Barley was malted for use in unlicensed alehouses; feed grains were diverted from the fowls. These statements were strictly the party line of Elizabeth and her Privy Council. But Lambarde knew better than to develop these issues in Kent, where the raising of barley and hops for beer and ale was a primary source of income. So he changed to the true issue that farmers were speculating in selling grain at a time of national crisis. He insisted that he was not exaggerating conditions. As the jurors well knew, they were bound by their oaths to report on these offenders who were profiting from withholding grain from the market. Finally, he recognized a basic point about maintaining law and order. If breaking the law seemed to benefit certain farmers with grain to sell at high prices, then other citizens would find other laws to break for their personal advantage. The result would be chaos if the whole system of the law should thus be broken bit by bit. So unless they wished this woeful result, which he himself could scarcely face, they dared not protect offenders in disobeying the laws against hoarding grain.

Later in that same year, in November, 1596, Lambarde presided over an Inquisition Post Mortem, for which the specific articles are unavailable. But his Charge to the Jurors mentioned the tenancy of a Mr. Clayton and also the tenancy extended to a Mr. Wyles by marriage. These personal references suggest that the jurors were acquainted with these individuals. So this particular Charge is distinctly personal rather than hortatory and abstract.

Lambarde explained very carefully the theory that the land resides in the possession of the sovereign from ancient times, by whatever variants of the fees. Hence in cases where treason and/or heresy prevailed, the land reverted to the Crown. In this case there were certain precedents established, since some of the property originally had descended to the heirs as land granted by knight's fee; other portions were originally in fee simple. The complications arose because the title to certain portions had passed through lease, sale, and mortgage. Yet without preservation of the actual articles, reconstruction of the case is impossible.

Lambarde had been through these intricate details in acquiring the farms for endowing his College for the Poor and he had traced many titles of land while acting as Burghley's deputy in the Alienations Office. As a common lawyer, too, he had dealt with these problems in presenting the evidence for countless Inquisitions Post Mortem. (It is exasperating to be unable to answer why he preserved this particular Charge to the Jurors, unless he regarded it as an example of how the minds of the jurors should be prepared to accept the justice in this final accounting of the deceased person's estate.)

While Lambarde was engaged in these practical matters of administering the estates of rich and powerful men, the Queen had lost in Rokeby and Cobham two of her most useful administrators. Burghley had turned over most of his duties at this time to his son Sir Robert Cecil. The young Earl of Essex was fascinating the aging Queen as a brilliant courtier and foolhardy general. Sir Walter Raleigh, now in eclipse, was writing his *Discovery of Guiana,* which was not to be published until some years later in 1606. Shakespeare's *Romeo and Juliet* carried idealized, youthful lovers to the never-never land of faraway Verona. And much to the Queen's pleasure, Edmund Spenser had finished three more books of his *The Faerie Queene.* It was an exciting time to be young, but Elizabeth was old. Already her courtiers were thinking of her successor, as her popularity diminished and the harsh realities of the future confronted the young and the timorous middle-aged.

In the Chancery Lambarde's work was increased by the reforms that Sir Thomas Egerton was instituting. As shown by letters, as yet unprinted, that Lambarde received from various litigants, there were two basic problems confronting this high court. Lawyers were demanding review of cases that they had lost in the courts of common law, if their clients were able to pay the costs of appeal, and the unrest of the time augmented the appeals of influential persons who sought summary dismissal of cases in which they had become involved in civil actions. The judges of the common law courts contended that the privileged courts, particularly the Star Chamber, described as a prerogative court, but also the Chancery and the Court of Requests, had extended their jurisdictions beyond the precedents established and were consequently intruding upon the jurisdictions of the common law courts. Both sides defended their positions with vigor and learning. Sir Edward Coke and Sir Francis Bacon in their individual ways were defending the theory and practice of the common law. Egerton, as Lord Keeper of the Great Seal, favored the prerogative of the Queen.

Lambarde's "Archeion" manuscript, if it had been printed

at this time, would quite probably have settled the issue, for as a history of the high courts, it dealt with the precedents and procedures of both the common law courts and the so-called prerogative courts. But Secretary Cecil, to whom it was dedicated, continued, now five years later, to withhold this manuscript from the printers.

Some lawyers estimated that cases in Chancery were delayed more than three years. So instead of becoming a court for quick and final action, Chancery had become as slow as the high courts of common law. Egerton sought to accelerate the work of the court, and Lambarde preserved two letters from this period that indicated the response to Egerton's endeavors. One case, involving the Abdy family, was represented by Thomas Derdent in a letter dated April 8, 1597. It emphasized the expense in the litigation carried through the common law courts to determination in the Chancery. It also illustrated the direct appeal to the judge presiding over the case. Even Lambarde was subjected to this very common procedure. In the case of Derdent, simple flattery was used.

Ten days after Egerton was appointed Lord Keeper, he appointed Lambarde Master of the Rolls, on May 26, 1597; in reality Lambarde's office was to serve as Egerton's deputy. Yet the designation remained, even if the Lord Keeper usually reserved the Mastership of the Rolls for himself. This office also placed the Master of the Rolls as President of the Chancery Division. So this was the highest recognition that could be given to Lambarde's knowledge of the law.

At this time Lambarde made his will, a long and detailed document that held certain provisions of interest to modern readers. For instance, Shakespearean scholars have made much of Shakespeare's leaving the second best bed to his wife and the best bed to his daughter. Lambarde made precisely this provision more than a dozen years earlier. Furthermore, he showed great concern for his daughter's marriage and dowry, when she should attain the age of eighteen. He then named four ladies to advise his daughter in making a suitable marriage. These persons were Mrs. Margery Windham, his brother's wife now remarried to Humphrey Windham, his lifelong friend from Lincoln's Inn; Mrs. Audrey Multon, his sister-in-law; Lady Mary Bergevennye (Abergavenny), previously Lady Mary Fane; and Lady Christian Leveson. The latter two were the wives of his close associates.

He also directed that the education of his three sons be supervised by his close friends and associates. Sir John Leveson was to care for Multon, the heir, and Francis Tress was to be the tutor; old Sir John Tyndall was to be responsible for Gore; Sir George Byng of Wrotham was to look after Fane, the other twin. But if any of these gentlemen should be unable to serve, then Humphrey Windham was to serve any or all of Lambarde's sons. Lambarde likewise followed his father in avoiding the limitations of primogeniture by providing precise descriptions of properties to be divided among his children. And he requested that Sir Thomas Egerton give "conscionable aid" in carrying out these provisions. The bowls, pots, silver spoons, and other household items, the objects to which his present wife or his daughter might attach sentiment, were carefully distributed. But the deep concern for the future security of his ten-year-old daughter indicated that he felt a special responsibility for her.

Shortly after his appointment to be Master of the Rolls in Chancery, Lambarde was made a Bencher by order of the Council of Lincoln's Inn. For several years he had served as an "associate of the Bench," but now he was of the Council:

William Lambarde, an Associate of this Bench, being one of her Ma(jesty's) Master of her Court in Chancery, of great reading, learning, and experience, as yt is well known to all those w(ho) are at this Council assembled, is by whole consent chosen one of the Bench of this Societie.[3]

This well-merited award came to Lambarde at the age of sixty-one, and to a man of his independence such recognition could only be highly gratifying. He had not sought favor. On the contrary, he had said and done many things of which his enemies could have taken full advantage.

At just this time in the Chancery the case of Coppin *vs.* Cranmer revealed Lambarde's independence. His associate on the bench, Sir John Tyndall, likewise revealed integrity in dealing with Lord Montjoy's intervention. Montjoy presumed to dictate the settlement of this suit in favor of his young friend George Cranmer, whom he wished to take with him to Ireland. Lord Montjoy, perhaps better known as the valiant soldier Captain Charles Blount, was involved with the Earl of Essex's expedition to capture the defiant Irish leader, the Earl of Tyrone.

Lambarde and Tyndall were unwilling to give summary dismissal to a complicated case. As the unprinted letters from Coppin show, the future of some unprotected children were involved, and Coppin asked for a new bill calling forth a new accounting of the estate with special consideration for the widow and children, one of whom was a lunatic. Under the *statute de praerogative regis*, the sovereign would take custody of the natural fool, but if the lunatic were judged to be an idiot then the wardship could be highly profitable. It was not a simple distinction confronting Lambarde and Tyndall. But as far as Cranmer was concerned, he was merely the proprietor of land, possibly inherited from the Archbishop of Canterbury, who had leased the lands to the Coppins. Finally, Lambarde and Tyndall filed a new bill favoring Coppin's contention, not that of Cranmer and the powerful Lord Montjoy.

Lambarde preserved a letter that he received from Dr. Styward, who opposed the new regulation in the Chancery for the publishing of witnesses at the beginning of the trial rather than during its progress. This was one of Egerton's endeavors to avoid delay and speed up cases in the Chancery. Dr. Styward had the audacity to threaten Lambarde with seeking relief from the Lord Keeper himself if Lambarde did not rescind the court order issued to him and Dr. Byng to present the names of witnesses.

These unprinted letters reveal how difficult it was for a Master in the Chancery to maintain his integrity and mete out justice to all. Lady Wharton sought through her attorney to excuse herself for seeming to attempt to bribe Lambarde. Her attorney was the distinguished Michael Moleyns, who explained that Lady Wharton, "being a woman," was unaware of her fault. He flattered Lambarde: "We will not willingly lose your good opinion of us in this question."

Meanwhile the Earl of Essex's expedition had come to grief, as he sought a compromise with Tyrone and his hungry soldiers returned to England in rags. The wily Secretary Robert Cecil had evidently intruded upon the Queen's provisions for her favorite and Essex was denied the food and ordnance that he had been faithfully promised.

Secretary Cecil was secretly engaging in correspondence with King James VI of Scotland, whose grandmother was the daughter of the first Tudor King, Henry VII. Although James's mother, Mary Queen of Scots, had been beheaded for treason, he appeared to be a more likely successor to Elizabeth than the English Stuart line represented by Allegra Stuart. Another woman on the throne was unthinkable at this time to the majority of Elizabeth's courtiers, who were corresponding with James VI of Scotland, maneuvering for preference in the new reign which might come at any time.

The Earl of Essex came home without honor but with faithful support from the minority of Elizabeth's peers led by the Earl of Southampton. Their strategy was to appeal to the citizens of London, arouse rebellion, and place Essex on the throne. For this purpose they revived Shakespeare's earlier play of *King Richard II* with the deposition scene. But the endeavor failed. Essex was captured and convicted of high treason; he was placed in the Tower of London and later beheaded.

Now Elizabeth was alone. The struggles of Egerton, Coke, Bacon, and Secretary Cecil concerned her only because she realized that their struggles for power were not for her. Cecil, since the death of his father in 1598, had played one man against the other with particular dislike for the one remaining courtier from the illustrious past, Sir Walter Raleigh. The Queen in her loneliness continued to remain the symbol of past glory, but Cecil was not his father; nor was the new Lord Cobham to be trusted with all the labors that she had given to his father. The devotion of Archbishop Parker, Thomas Wotton, Sir Francis Walsingham, and Lord Burghley, not to mention the peculiar place in her esteem held by the Earl of Leicester, had died with the old order. The new advisers offered lip-service and anxiously awaited her death.

Lambarde, too, was very much alone, except for his chief, the Lord Keeper. Yet he seemed to be making progress with his compilation of important cases from the files in Chancery. The important book known as *Cary's Reports* remains associated with Lambarde only to those who read the title page, where full acknowledgment was given to his labors.

Perhaps Lambarde, too, had become a symbol of the past, for he was called upon to address the jurors at the spring quarter sessions held at Maidstone on April 1, 1600. And on this occasion he spoke like an elder statesman, from the vantage point of years of experience, reminding the jurors once again that maintenance of the peace was in their hands. Changing times had not destroyed the pith of his message: the realm must be protected from the enemies within. And only the inquiring jurors could report the offenders. The good laws and the evil offenders were still matters of good and evil. The body politic depended upon the punishment of those persons who committed felonies and misdemeanors. The order of the kingdom of the bees and the protection of the lambs from the savage beasts were obvious examples. And he ended with the statement made in the preface to his first book, *Archaionomia,* that nations which were destroyed had first iniquity within them that opened the way to destruction.

The manuscript of this Charge to the Jurors shows that Lambarde had given great care to the writing and revision of this address, and in looking back after more than 350 years, one recognizes that it summed up his belief that the law was indeed like the wall protecting a house. His antiquarian studies and his wide reading of history "both divine and profane" had convinced him that no man, even the brilliant Essex, could take the law into his own hands for his own advantage without destroying the realm. And Shakespeare in his great chronicle plays—from the usurpation of the throne of King Richard II down to King Henry VII— had demonstrated in his pageants of the War of the Roses the chaos that followed disobedience of the law. But Lambarde's words were not for the millions of theater goers in later centuries. Perhaps a few more than a hundred auditors listened, but, though unheeded, he also spoke to later generations.

Queen Elizabeth appointed Lambarde to be Keeper of the Rolls in the Tower of London on January 21, 1601. Perhaps she finally recognized that he was the remaining associate of the great peers who had served her with devotion. Whatever her reason for bestowing this honor, it was royal recognition long overdue. She asked him to make an index of the records kept in the Tower. There were few competent for this task, and scarcely a competent person alive, except Lambarde, who would take the time and pains for accomplishing it.

Lambarde paused in the spring to write one more charge to the Jurors to be uttered that spring at the quarter sessions in Maidstone, but the manuscript was inscribed, "not used."

Finally in August he completed this Index of the Rolls and entitled it *Pandecta Rotulorum.* But instead of requesting an audience with Her Majesty, he asked the Countess of Warwick to deliver his work to the Queen. Probably he still remained the loyal but stubborn servant of Her Majesty in this action. For Lady Warwick, the wife of Ambrose Dudley, had become rather notorious for her acceptance of fees for intercession with Elizabeth. With Lady Edmonds, who had once refused as too small the amount of £100 for intervention in a case pending in the Chancery, Lady Warwick had taken advantage of the old Queen's friendship.[4] Now Lambarde certainly had heard of these fees, and he had demonstrated his own disdain for this common practice. So he might well have given his *Pandecta Rotulorum* to Lady Warwick, not in modesty but in protest against such intervention. At the end of his time, he had no need for patronage.

Queen Elizabeth invited him to her privy chamber in Greenwich Palace and he of course accepted. She began the interview with the declaration that if "any subject of mine do me a service, I will thankfully accept it from his own hands." She then opened his book and began to read the Latin, saying, "You shall see that I can read." Then she took up a number of Latin words in his text and asked for the legal significance in their use.

When she came to the rolls dealing with the reign of King Richard II, she said, "I am Richard II, know ye not that?"

Lambarde replied, "Such a wicked imagination was determined and attempted by a most unkind Gent(leman), the most adorned creature that ever your Majestie made." Whereupon she replied, "He that will forget God, will also forget his benefactors; this tragedy was played 40tie times in open streets and houses."

Her loneliness and her need to speak to someone whom she could trust obviously moved Lambarde deeply, for he returned home and wrote out this conversation. Perhaps it was even a greater tribute to his integrity than the award of the office in the Tower for her thus to confide in him.

The Queen then resumed her questioning of the legal significance of numerous other Latin words in the *Pandecta Rotulorum,* thereby showing her personal interest in work that might have been neglected by her. She praised the precision and learning in Lambarde's work, and then she observed: "In those days force and arms did prevail; but now the wit of the fox is everywhere on foot, so as hardly a faithful or vertuouse man may be found."

Then she dismissed him, saying, "Farewell good and honest Lambarde."

Perhaps this accolade has lost its savor, but "good and honest" recognized Lambarde's integrity, for these words then meant "virtuous and honorable." He had indeed not forgotten his God and his conduct was not merely honest but honorable.

Two weeks later he died, on August 19, 1601, in Westcombe Manor, East Greenwich, Kent, and was buried in the parish church of East Greenwich. There against the south wall a monument was erected to his memory bearing this inscription:

William Lambarde, of Lincoln's Inn, some time Master in Chancery, Keeper of the Rolls and Records, of the office of Alienations to Queen Elizabeth, founded the College of the poor of Greenwich, and endowed it. Obiit 1601, Aug. 19, at Westcombe in East Greenwich.

* * *

At the time of William Lambarde's death, Multon Lambarde was seventeen, a year younger than his father was at the time of his father's death. Multon Lambarde married and continued to reside in Westcombe Manor. It was his son Thomas who took great interest in William Lambarde and his reputation. When the old church in East Greenwich was to be torn down to build the present structure there, Thomas decided to have his grandfather's remains transferred to the parish church in Sevenoaks. He also removed the monument and erected another plaque with the lettering in gilt on black marble:

Hic situs est Gulielmus Lambarde, Londiensis, in hospito jure consultorum Lincolniensi paredrus; in alma cancellaria magister; ad tempus custos rotulorum infra Turrim London. Ab Alienationibus (quas vocant) augustissimae Anglorum reginae Elizabethae, eujus sacrae memoriae et nomini consecratum suo sumptu solus, et fundavit et annus redituo dotavit collegium pauperum Greenovici in Cantia. Obiit anno Domini 1601, Augusti 19° die, apud Wescombe, in East Greenwiche.

Archaionomia 1568	Justice of the Peace 1581[0]
Perambulation of Kent	Pandecta Rotulorum 1600[1]
1579[6]	Archeion 1591

Thus Thomas gave a memorial to his grandfather more proper perhaps in Latin as befitted a Latin scholar than the simple prose statement made by Lambarde's heir, Multon.

The confusion of dates for the *Archeion* and *Pandecta Rotulorum* lacks interest by comparison with the translation of *Eirenarcha*.

It was Thomas Lambarde, the grandson, who some thirty-two years later published *Archeion,* apparently to repudiate an unauthorized edition in that year.

Today the visitor to the parish church in Sevenoaks finds, at the base of the ancient tower, this notice:

> This part of the north aisle, viz. from this spot to the first pillar to the buttress of the steeple being 264 square feet is the chancel of the Lambarde family.

This statement is signed by the rector and two church wardens. Beyond in the north wall of the church is a large memorial window with colored glass with the following inscription:

> In memory of William Lambarde Keeper of the records in the Tower to Queen Elizabeth 1st and founder of the Queen Elizabeth Almhouses of Greenwich, and of his descendents who lived and owned land in West Kent since his time and have resided in the parish of Sevenoaks since 1654. This window is erected by Debora Campbell daughter of William Gore Lambarde 1954.

Hence it was three hundred years earlier that Thomas Lambarde, the grandson of the perambulator and legal historian, began the series of memorials to this family in the ancient Sevenoaks church still maintained in excellent repair. For in this "chancel of the Lambarde family" appear numerous plaques and memorials of varied kind to members of the family throughout these three centuries.

EPILOGUE

In retrospect, Lambarde's fitness for high office in the Chancery appears to have been the logical reward for devoting his life to the administration of justice with equity. Certainly no other lawyer or jurist knew as much about court procedures and jurisdictions as the author of the recently completed manuscript entitled "Archeion." Now he was to have the fullest opportunity as a Master in the Chancery to adjudicate the kinds of cases in which he was chiefly interested. So it is rather easy to assume that a pattern of conduct was fulfilled in Lambarde's life.

In the mystery of human attainment, however, there seems to be a delicate balance between character and coincidence in events, unless one has a strong predilection for recognizing destiny. In the case of Lambarde, twenty-four years had passed since that day in Lincoln's Inn when he and John Puckering had together received the call to the bar. At that time both appeared to be outstanding young men who would bring honor to their country and to Lincoln's Inn. But the fact that makes Lambarde's career interesting, regardless of his attaining high office and writing important books, is the development of his character under the pressure of events over which he had no control.

Despite the logical development of Lambarde's career as a scholar, fortuitous circumstances gave him opportunity for further distinction. Two of his fellow students at Lincoln's

Inn became Lords Keeper of the Great Seal, and were thus in a position to advance Lambarde's reputation. Puckering chose Lambarde for the Chancery and Egerton named him Master of the Chancery Rolls. The pattern, from Anglo-Saxon and Latin manuscripts to Latin manuscripts in the closing years, would suggest an appropriate conclusion for Lambarde, an expert in manuscripts from the beginning to the end of his career. If one follows this pattern and looks again to Lambarde's years in Lincoln's Inn, it would be as reasonable to say that he had directed his life to becoming Master of the Rolls, and consequently that he had achieved his lifelong ambition because of Sir William Cordell's influence upon him. In those early days, Cordell, the Latin and Anglo-Saxon scholar, held a high place in Lambarde's regard, and Cordell was Master of the Rolls. One remembers that Lambarde dedicated *Archaionomia* to Sir William Cordell, rather than to Laurence Nowell who shared his Anglo-Saxon manuscripts with young Lambarde, and not to Archbishop Parker, the leader in the revival of Anglo-Saxon learning and later Lambarde's patron. Yet it was Cordell to whom the book was dedicated, and it was in honor of Cordell that Lambarde later gave to the Drapers' Company of London an exquisite silver cup decorated with Cordell's coat-of-arms. If one dared to speculate about early influences on Lambarde, Cordell would surely be foremost and his office as Master of the Rolls would then become Lambarde's goal. But the facts scarcely warrant such interpretation. And if they did support this assumption, then Lambarde would have to be regarded merely as an ambitious man.

After being called to the bar, Lambarde did not proceed to climb the ladder of the legal hierarchy. On the contrary, he sojourned in Kent, developing his acquaintanceship with another Lincoln's Inn man, Thomas Wotton, and learning from him a vast store of Kentish lore. Lambarde gained much practical information about farming and the value of land from George Multon with whom he resided for many years in St. Cleres, Ightham. This was not the course to the Chancery, much less to the office of Master of the Rolls. Yet all of the information that Lambarde gained about practical matters in Kent, along with his peregrinations in the fields and woods and study of ancient manuscripts, became useful years later.

The fullness of his experience undoubtedly did mold Lambarde's character, for he had resources when adversity struck him. Just suppose that his topographical history of England had been more advanced than Camden's, and Camden rather than Lambarde had given up the project. The years ahead in antiquarian research would not have permitted Lambarde to enter the Commission of the Peace in Kent immediately. He would have been traveling and note-taking in other counties. But such was not his destiny. There was also the cruel death of his young wife, Multon's daughter. Had she lived and borne him a household of children, would he then have given away in middle age half his fortune to build and endow his College for the Poor of Queen Elizabeth? He was a generous man, but not irresponsible. But the way in which he accepted adversity revealed his character. Even if he gained strength and purpose for his life from these difficult experiences, he certainly did not choose this course to the Chancery.

If he became interested in the Commission of the Peace while living with George Multon, a justice of the peace, and turned to the early, authentic records from which to write a history, then he would seem to have been a likely candidate for the office of justice of the peace. Probably no one who knew Lambarde's abilities would ever have considered that his becoming a justice of the peace was any fulfillment of his mind and heart. Yet by writing *Eirenarcha*, he lifted this often satirized office to dignity and established a uniform set of procedures for handling the new statutes enacted by Parliament. From his experience in hearing and determining cases, he found another need, a handbook for the parish officers, *The Duties of Constables, Borsholders, Tythingmen, and such other lowe Ministers of the Peace.* Next he became interested in the jurors and wrote long and intricate Charges to prepare their minds for their sacred duties. An oath before God was not to be entered into lightly and casually, which was the situation that he found while plunging into the problem of justice with equity in local government.

In reviewing the cases that Lambarde heard and determined, and in recalling the admonitions to the jurors to be mindful of the significance of their oaths taken before God, the impression cannot be denied that Lambarde was something of a reformer, a priest on the bench, rather than a common lawyer who had become a jurist. His enormous enthusiasm for his work was the manifestation of patriotic fervor that triumphed over the disillusionment of the era. Whether this spirit of patriotism became apparent in Shakespeare's chronicle history plays, Spenser's poem in celebration of Glorianna, Holinshed's *Chronicles,* or Camden's *Britannia,* it developed from the awakening of pride in England and the heritage of being an Englishman. Call it a surging spirit of nationalism. The writers, merchants, and officers in government felt it and talked about it. This consciousness of heritage became manifest in the revival of Anglo-Saxon customs, laws, and literature, of which Lambarde's *Archaionomia* was an expression. The pride in the island, its geographical formation, its history of Anglo-Saxon and Roman institutions and towns, led Lambarde to the writing of *A Perambulation of Kent.* And the sense of heritage likewise became clear in *Archeion,* the history of the high courts in England with emphasis upon their separateness from the

Roman courts and imperial law. On the other hand, his handbooks, *Eirenarcha* and *The Duties of Constables,* did improve
standards in legal procedures by reminding justices and
parish officers that their service was in an honorable tradition.

Yet as an author, Lambarde did not write for the public,
influential though his books were on learned men in his
time and even though his two handbooks had wide distribution among men who were not knowledgeable in legal matters.
But his integrity, manifest in his books, his work with the
jurors, and his administrative activities, stands out as achievement in itself. Nevertheless the inner man was not a person
enhanced by great public office; on the contrary, the inner
man enhanced the offices to which he was appointed. So it
was Lambarde's character, his integrity and earnestness that
made him the person, in whom Queen Elizabeth's confiden-
tial advisers—Archbishop Parker, Thomas Wotton, Lord
Burghley, Lord Cobham—and finally Elizabeth herself,
placed an absolute trust.

The record shows that he did not stop studying and writing even though he was hampered in his last years by dimmed
eyesight and illness. He gained joy in learning and found
practical applications for his knowledge. His "Ephemeris"
reveals how active he was between the age of forty-five and
fifty-four when he was studying and writing at the height of
his zeal. All these things, then, added up to comprise the
store of learning and experience which finally brought him
recognition and awards of post of honor and trust during the
closing ten years of his life.

From the activities of Lambarde's life it is obvious that he
was indeed a paradoxical character able to concentrate one day
on details of legal scholarship and rush forth the next day to
examine a felon who had stolen a sheep or a silver spoon.
And perhaps it is here that his character becomes fully dis-
closed in all its complexity. He had a great zest for living,

usually manifest in Elizabethan days by hard drinking, wenching, and campaigns to the Azores or Ireland. Although his interests were widely diverted, his energy was channeled into a desire to bring justice and order to human existence. He found in the law a definite ethic based on the Ten Commandments. And to the end of his life, he continued to preach to the jurors that peace and order rested within their own hands if only they would follow the dictates of conscience.

Lambarde's love of England and his religious faith combined to make both his utterances and his writings convincing to practical men in the marketplace and on farms. But his usefulness in local government scarcely appears to be the ladder any man in middle age could assume as the way to the Chancery. Among the hundreds of justices of the peace in various counties, he became the one Elizabethan justice symbolic of what the office could mean to persons of high estate in government as well as the lowliest oaf wandering along the old Watling-Street Road in Kent. Such integrity and learning and experience were needed in the Chancery and, perhaps strangely enough in political life, Lambarde's contribution was recognized in time for him to give his talents fullest expression. Here was a man who found in the administration a practical means by which England advanced to a realization of equal justice for rich and poor alike while religious controversy, war, and an expanding economy were changing the traditional ways of life on that island. William Lambarde brought the Tudor dream of local government a step or two closer to reality, a concept close to the heart of Queen Elizabeth I, for the glory of English law and order.

NOTES

Chapter 2

1. John Nichols, ed., *Bibliotheca Topographica Britannica*, I, 493–532. Joseph Jackson Howard, ed., *Miscellanea Genealogica et Heraldica*, II, 98–102. Edward Hasted, *A History and Topographical Survey of the County of Kent*, I, 51–2. *Archaeologia Cantiana*, V, 247–56. Daniel Lyson, *The Environs of London*, IV, 460, 480, 483. John Stow, *A Survey of London*, Everyman edition, p. 470. A. H. Thomas and I. D. Thornley, eds., *The Great Chronicle of London*, pp. 10, 193, 202, 270, 427.

2. A. H. Johnson, *The History of the Worshipful Company of Drapers*, II, 179–80.

3. Hasted, *Kent*, I, 52, 145. Stow, *Survey*, p. 183.

4. *Arch. Cant.*, V, 247–56.

5. Thomas and Thornley, *Chronicle*, pp. 196, 202, 429.

6. Death of John Lambarde: Stow, *Survey*, III, 80; *Arch. Cant.*, V, 247; John G. Nichols, ed., *The Diary of Henry Machyn*, p. 67.

7. Wills of John and Alice Lambarde: *Arch. Cant.*, V, 256.

8. Joel Hurstfield, *The Queen's Wards*, pp. 3, 5, 20.

9. J. Howard Brown, *Elizabethan Schooldays*, pp. 7–8, 54. A. F. Leach, *Educational Charters and Documents*, pp. xxxviii, 416. A. F. Leach, "St. Paul's School Before Colet," *Arch. Cant.*, LXIII, 191. Edward Haviland Miller, *The Professional Writer in Elizabethan England*, pp. 35–6. Foster Watson, *The English Grammar Schools to 1600*, pp. 155, 534–5. Louis B. Wright, *Middle-Class Culture in Elizabethan England*, pp. 21–34, 43–80. Johnson, *Drapers*, I, 98, note 3; II, 106, 1021, 1029.

10. C. E. Mallet, *A History of the University of Oxford*, II, 17, 121–3; concerning Horne or Hearne: I, 84, 220.

Chapter 3

1. J. D. Walker and W. P. Baildon, *The Black Books, The Records of the Honorable Society of Lincoln's Inn*, I, 62.

2. Sir George Buck, *The Third Universitie of England.*

3. "Collectanae of Laurence Nowell and William Lambarde," *Bibliotheca Topographica Britannica*, I, 510–12. Robert Flower, "Lawrence Nowell and the Discourse of England in Tudor Times," *The Proceedings of the British Academy*, XXI, 47–73. Ralph Churton, *The Life of Alexander Nowell, Dean of St. Paul's;* for Laurence Nowell, pp. 233, 236–7.

4. John Lord Campbell, *The Lives of the Lord Chancellors. Black Books*, I, 356, 393, 412.

5. John Nichols, *The Progresses and Public Processions of Queen Elizabeth*, III, 581–5. Samuel E. Thorne, ed., *A Discourse upon the Exposicions & Understanding of Statutes*, p. 42.

6. J. R. Dasent, ed., *Acts of the Privy Council.* I. S. Leadam, *Select Cases in the Court of Requests.*

7. *Black Books*, II, 366, 397, 398, 400, 405, 409, 419, 457.

8. *Ibid.*, pp. 14, 17, 86 105.

9. Sir John Neale *The Elizabethan House of Commons*, p. 363. See also: Conyers Read, *William Lambarde and Local Government*, p. 8, note 16; Conyers Read, *Mr. Secretary Cecil and Queen Elizabeth*, p. 365.

10. *Black Books*, I, 388. "Revels at Lincoln's Inn, 1566," *The Progresses of Queen Elizabeth*, I, 251–2.

11. *Black Books*, I, 457.

12. Virgil B. Heltzel, "Sir Thomas Egerton and William Lambard," *Huntington Library Quarterly*, XI (1947–8), 201–3.

13. Sir William Holdsworth says of Lambarde's *Archaionomia:* "as pioneer in an unknown land, his work was good." See: K. Sisam, "The Authenticity of Certain Texts in Lambarde's 'Archaionomia' 1568," *MLR*, XX (1925), 253–69; *MLR*, VIII (1923), 100–3; Felix Liebermann, "Gesetze der Angelsachsen," *Anglia*, July, 1924, pp. 214 ff.; F. L. Attenborough, ed., *The Laws of the Earliest English Kings;* David C. Douglas, *English Scholars*, p. 82; Henry Lévy-Ullman, *The English Legal Tradition*, p. 18; Felix Hull, "The Costumal of Kent," *Archaeologia Cantiana*, LXXIII, 148–59.

Chapter 4

1. For the range of Wotton's friends and information, see D. Eland, ed., *Thomas Wotton's Letter-Book.*

2. The pedigree of the Multon family as recorded by Lambarde appears in *Archaeologia Cantiana*, V, 243–8.

3. John Nichols, *The Progresses and Public Processions of Queen Elizabeth*, I, 325–7.

4. Edward Hasted, *A History and Topographical Survey of the County of Kent*, XII, 312.

5. John Strype, *The Life and Acts of Matthew Parker*, III, 267.

6. See *Ibid.*, II, 292, letter to Lord Burghley for what happened during July of 1573, although this letter is usually dated June 27, 1573.

7. A. A. Arnold, "Cobham College," *Arch. Cant.*, XXVII, 64–109. A. A. Arnold, "Cobham and Its Manors," *Arch. Cant.*, XXVII, 110–35.

8. John Nichols, ed., *Bibliotheca Topographica Britannica*, I, 498.

9. "A Form of Morning and Evening Prayer," *Bib. Top. Brit.*, I, 513–14.

10. *Arch. Cant.*, XXXIX, 158–9. See A. H. Johnson, *The History of the Worshipful Company of Drapers*, II, 526, note 1.

11. Hasted, *Kent*, II, 366.

12. *The Progresses of Queen Elizabeth*, II, 561–3.

13. "Extracts from the Statutes of the College for the Poor of Queen Elizabeth," *Bib. Top. Brit.*, I, 516.

14. I am indebted to Dr. Felix Hull for sending to the Folger Shakespeare Library a photostatic copy of this unprinted essay, probably intended to be used in Lambarde's projected survey of England. Here is the heading of it: "Elucidarious Angliae, sive Tetraphonia Propriorum Nomium, Populorum, Urbium, Oppidorium, Fluminorum, Montium, Caesterorum locum Angliae quae passim in Historiis leguntur Commentarius ex optimis quibus que scriptoribus collectus, opera Gulielmi Lambarde, 1577."

15. *Bib. Top. Brit.*, I, 512.

16. J. D. Walker and W. P. Baildon, *The Black Books, The Records of the Honorable Society of Lincoln's Inn*, I, 412.

Chapter 5

1. All references in this chapter to Lambarde's day-by-day activities, between 1580 and 1588, are from his "Ephemeris," which can be found in Conyers Read, ed., *William Lambarde and Local Government*.

2. Act of Parliament (5 Eliz. c. 18). When Queen Elizabeth I appointed Nicholas Bacon, a respected lawyer and the brother-in-law of William Cecil (later Lord Burghley), as Lord Keeper of the Great Seal, she gave a patent with her warrant declaring him to have the same powers as if Lord Chancellor. But as questions arose concerning his authority, Parlia-

ment enacted a detailed statute making indubitably clear the full extent "to all intents, constructions, and purposes as if the same Keeper of the Great Seal for the time being were Lord Chancellor of England." Hence in subsequent appointments by Queen Elizabeth I, complete power of this office remained, regardless of the title: 1579, Sir Thomas Bromley, Lord Chancellor; 1587, Sir Christopher Hatton, Lord Chancellor; 1591, Sir John Puckering, Lord Keeper of the Great Seal; 1596, Sir Thomas Egerton, Lord Keeper of the Great Seal. See John Lord Campbell, *The Lives of the Lord Chancellors*, II, 100-1, 197.

3. According to the "Memoir" in *Bibliotheca Topographica Britannica*, p. 499, Lambarde was appointed a justice of the peace in 1579. Much of this difficulty arises from the condition that Lambarde used the old style, among the three calendars in use, from January into March. See: J. B. Black, *The Reign of Queen Elizabeth*, p. 269; Bertram Osborne, *Justices of the Peace;* Michael Dalton, *The Country Justice;* T. G. Barnes and A. Hassell Smith, "Justices of the Peace from 1558-1668, a Revised List of Sources," *Bulletin of Historical Research*, XXXII (1959), 121-242; Sir James Fitzjames Stephen, *A History of the Criminal Law of England*.

4. The first edition of Eirenarcha and its reprintings have stimulated two scholars to examine manuscripts in Lambarde's library. Elizabeth Lamond collated Lambarde's copy of *A Discourse of the Common Weal of this Realm of England* with that in the Bodleian Library (Add. C. 273) and found that the latter was free from scribal errors and represented a revised and improved text (Cambridge, 1893, p. xxxii). Although she did not live long enough to complete her work, W. Cunningham supplied the required footnotes. F. J. Furnivall edited *William Stafford's Compendious or briefe Examination of certayne ordinary Complaints of our Countrymen in these our Dayes, A.D. 1581.* Furnivall did not inquire about the authorship, since for him "W. S." meant William Stafford.

More recently, Edward Hughes has dissented from Dr. Lamond's ascription of this work to John Hales, pointing out evidence from two additional manuscripts in the Marquis of Salisbury's collection and in the Yelverton collection. Hughes favored Smith, thinking of the nephew, not the son, of Sir Thomas Smith, as "W. S."

Lambarde's copy contained this note: "Note, that this booke was published in printe under the title of A Briefe Conceipt of Inglishe policie by one W. S. in the yeare 1581, whereas it was long synce penned by Sir Thomas Smythe (as some say), or Mr. Iohn Hales (as others thinke) eyther in the reigne of H(enry) VIII or E(dward) VI. And I myselfe have long had this copy of it which I caused to be written out in the yeare 1565." Lambarde's comments indicate that he was not only shrewd and learned but, like the author of *The Common Weal of this Realm of England*, thinking in classical terms about the problem. So a meeting of minds took place between the author of this tract and Lambarde, the practical man concerned with the land. The importance of this background to the writing of *Eirenarcha* cannot be overstated in considering Lambarde's books and manuscripts.

The various printings and editions of *Eirenarcha* provide a bibliographical problem of some dimensions. For example, Sir William Holdsworth, in the Appendix to Vol. IV of *A History of English Law*, reproduces both the contents of *Eirenarcha* and "The Articles of the Charge Given by the Justices of the Peace at Quarter Sessions." This procedure recognizes, as does his discussion (pp. 117–19), the importance of Lambarde's contribution and suffices very well indeed for the history of the law. But the book Holdsworth describes and praises for its organization is the edition of 1619; this edition appeared eighteen years after Lambarde's death and represented the culmination of many revisions and additions to the book. The significance of the date is that the precedents do not appear in the first printings of *Eirenarcha* but in the edition of 1588.

The evolution of *Eirenarcha*, its sources and revisions, receives full treatment in two studies by Bertha Haven Putnam: (1) *Early Treatises on the Practice of the Justice of the Peace in the Fifteenth and Sixteenth Centuries*, Vol. VII, and (2) "The Earliest Form of Lambard's 'Eirenarcha' and a Kent Wage Assessment of 1563," *EHR*, XLI (1926), 260–73. Dr. Putnam analyzes Lambarde's sources and authorities cited by him and also Crompton to reach the opinion that they "had availed themselves of practically all the legal literature in print important for their subject" (*Early Treatises*, p. 113). But this study becomes concerned primarily with Thomas Marowe and "His reading of the Peace in 1503" (*Early Treatises*, Chapter V). Obviously Dr. Putnam's intent was to place Lambarde's *Eirenarcha* in the development of books about the office of the Justice of the Peace with particular emphasis upon Marowe's work. But shortly after her book appeared in print, "The sale at a London auction in June 1924 of 'Manuscripts and books originally owned by William Lambarde, Historian of Kent (1536–1601)'" was the final step in the dispersion of what had been one of the most notable Elizabethan libraries. In particular she became interested in the "Module," the manuscript (Brit. Add. MS. 41137) which she analyzes in careful detail. She then found that this work corresponds to Lambarde's description of it in the "Epistle Dedicatorie" to Lord Chancellor Bromley dated "From Lincolnes Inne, this 27. day of

Ianuarie: 1581." After some questioning of Lambarde's rapid work in composing this "Module" after Bromley had indicated his intention of appointing Lambarde to the Commission of the Peace, she proceeds to the analysis of the first edition of *Eirenarcha* and finds that its organization compares with that of the "Module." Now she turns to the 1588 edition, with the precedents, and finds that Book I of the first edition becomes divided into three books and "the original Book II into Book IV." This is of course the division to which scholars using the editions after 1588 usually refer without considering the first edition. Next she concerns herself with Marowe's *De Pace*, upon which she had lavished so much attention in her earlier study of the books about the Justice of the Peace. Then she takes up the manuscript of John Goldwell's "Justices of the Peace," preserved and sold at auction with Lambarde's papers. She then notes: "If Mr. Hodgson (of the firm offering the Lambarde books and papers at auction) is right in his identification of some notes in the volume as written by Laurence Nowell (who shared his Anglo-Saxon legal manuscripts with Lambarde at Lincoln's Inn) who died in 1576, Goldsmith's treatise must have been begun several years before the 'Module.'" She then quotes Lambarde's "scornful remarks" and suggests two hypotheses detrimental to Lambarde's reputation: Was he familiar with Goldsmith's manuscript before he completed the "Module"? Did Goldsmith's work suggest either the manual or the need for an elaborate abridgement? These questions are not clearly separated in Miss Putnam's statements of them, but her intent is clear that she suspects Lambarde of indebtedness to Goldsmith's work for the suggestion of what he himself might do. She quotes Lambarde's "scornful remarks": "This woorke was not muche laboured by the author, for, besides a fewe things taken out of Mr. Fitzherberts book of the peace, and a light collection out of Mr. Stanfordes please of the Corone, it conteyneth no great matter; and was therefore refused when it was offered to the printer."

5. The popularity of Lambarde's *Eirenarcha* has been discussed in two rather recent books: W. W. Greg, *Some Aspects and Problems of London Publishing Between 1550 and 1650*, p. 59, and Percy Simpson, *Studies in Elizabethan Drama*, p. 182. Simpson quoted from Greg's earlier study of the *Records*, indicating a legal dispute between R. Tottell and C. Barker versus R. Newbery and H. Bynneman, dated January 15, 1582. Newbery and Bynneman were to print the first impression of 1,500 copies and give Tottell and Barker each fifty copies. Further editions were to be printed at the equal charge of all four; that is, Newbery and Bynneman were to publish at the assignment of Tottell and Barker. Simpson makes the point:

"The wide scope of the privilege appears from its being held to cover works like Lambarde's *Eirenarcha* and *The Duties of Constables,* and to define it Tottell made an entry in 1583 of what appears to be his entire stock" (*Studies,* p. 182).

6. David Cecil, *Two Quiet Lives,* pp. 48–9.

7. Richard Crompton's revision and enlargement of *LOffice et aucthoritie de Iustice de peace* had two prefatory statements: one was addresses to Sir Thomas Bromley, the other to all Crompton's associates in the Middle Temple, "Que svnt Iustices de Peace."

8. John S. Burns, ed., *The Star Chamber,* p. 75. A copy of the court order, dated May 16, 1582, dealing with the execution of Stephen Vallenger, is in the Folger Shakespeare Library.

Chapter 6

1. Conyers Read, ed., *William Lambarde and Local Government,* p. 50, note 3. See also, Allegra Woodworth, *Purveyance in the Royal Household* (Transactions of the American Philosophical Society, new series, XXXV, Pt. I, 40–1, 81).

2. References in this chapter to Lambarde's Charges to the Jurors can be found in Conyers Read, ed., *William Lambarde and Local Government.*

3. This edition brought the organization of the book into the division with four books, familiar to historians and lawyers who refer to *Eirenarcha.* But, for the record, there were reissues of the first edition of 1581 in 1582 and 1583, with the original division into two books. The text of the 1588 edition was enlarged to 629 pages, 118 more than in the first edition. This edition included: the Table of Statutes; a "Table of all the Principal Matters and Words"; an Appendix dealing with precedents, sundry inditements, presentments, and processes, dealing with all manner of criminal cases, from bugging to wearing silk.

4. G. S. Thomson, ed., *The Twysden Lieutenancy Papers,* p. 72.

5. Garrett Mattingly, *The Armada,* pp. 257 ff.

6. The folded, quarto-like manuscript of Lambarde's essay on the Alienations Office, now in the Folger Shakespeare Library, ends one sentence earlier than the text printed in Basil Montague's edition of *The Works of Francis Bacon,* XIII, 304 ff. Lambarde's manuscript has a crossed-out paragraph, almost a page in length, signed by him in Anglo-Saxon characters and dated "9 Maij 1595." Lambarde's manuscript has folded within it another manuscript entitled "A declaration of the yearely profites raysed by

sundrie deputies in this Office, since the first erection thereof: Collected by
Thomas Dudley, John Dudley, John Nuthall, and Jason Chomely, Deputies, 18 Elizabeth Reg." An annual table of receipts, the eighteenth through
the thirty-seventh year of Her Majesty's reign, lists the income derived
from this office. Another manuscript within the folds of the essay is entitled
"For a drafte. Whereof and to the end that all be not sondenly charged
with infidelitie and corruption." In Spedding, Ellis, and Heath, eds., *The
Letters and Life of Francis Bacon*, II, 120–1, the editors find, however,
that the brief history of the "Discourse of the Office for the Composition
of Alienations" should not be ascribed to Francis Bacon but to William
Lambarde. Although in 1730 Blackbourn had included this paper among
Bacon's works on the basis of a manuscript found in the library of the
Inner Temple, Spedding himself found a manuscript with similar title in
the library of Lincoln's Inn, signed by William Lambarde. Later Spedding
found a volume in the library of Cambridge University, signed in Anglo-
Saxon characters by William Lambarde, although this copy appeared to be
a first draft of the essay. Hence Spedding, recognizing the authenticity
of these signatures, assigned the essay to William Lambarde. See also Paul
L. Ward, "William Lambarde's Collections on Chancery," *Harvard University Bulletin*, VII (1953), 271–98.

7. William Lambarde, *Archeion*, pp. 154–76. *The Stationers's Register*
records under date of 1635 that on March 27 a book called Archion was
entered against the name of Daniel Frère as printer; that on July 1 this
entry was cancelled and replaced by an entry in the names of Master Seile
and Daniel Frère for the same book, but now called *Archeion, or, A
Discourse upon the High Courts of Justice in England*, "being the true
originall Copie from the Authors executor." There are two copies of the
manuscript in the Folger Shakespeare Library, 15143 and 15144.

Chapter 7

1. The unprinted letters in the Folger Shakespeare Library represent the
endeavors of various petitioners for Lambarde's aid while he was Master in
the Chancery: Anne Peckham, Robert Adams, George Byng, Thomas
Derdent, George Coppin, Dr. Stywarde, Michael Molyns.

Chapter 8

1. A. A. Arnold, "Cobham College," *Archaeologia Cantiana*, XXVII,
64–109. A. A. Arnold, "Cobham and Its Manors," *Arch. Cant.*, XXVII,

110–35. A. F. Allen, "An Early Poor Law Account," *Arch. Cant.*, LXIV, 74–84.

2. J. Payne Collier, ed., *The Egerton Papers*, pp. 228–9, 308–12.

3. J. D. Walker and W. P. Baildon, *The Black Books, The Records of the Honorable Society of Lincoln's Inn*, II, 51. "Councill of June 14, 1597."

4. Sir John Neale, "The Elizabethan Political Scene," *Essays in Elizabethan History*, p. 65.

BIBLIOGRAPHY

Lambarde Family

Archaeologia Cantiana, Vol. V (1863), Vol. XXXIX (1927).

Fry, E. A., ed. *Inquisitions Post Mortem for London, Tudor Period 1577–1603.* London, 1908.

Hasted, Edward. *A History and Topographical Survey of the County of Kent.* 4 vols. Canterbury, 1778–99.

Howard, Joseph Jackson, ed. *Miscellanea Genealogica et Heraldica.* London, 1876. Vol. II.

Johnson, A. H. *The History of the Worshipful Company of Drapers.* 5 vols. Oxford, 1914–22.

Lyson, Daniel. *The Environs of London, Being an Historical Account.* 4 vols. London, 1746, 1846. Vol. IV.

Nichols, John. *The Progresses and Public Processions of Queen Elizabeth, Illustrated with Historical Notes.* . . . 4 vols., London, 1788–1821; 3 vols., 1823.

——, ed. *Bibliotheca Topographica Britannica.* London, 1876. Vol. I.

Nichols, John G., ed. *The Diary of Henry Machyn, Citizen and Merchant-Taylor of London, 1550–63.* London, 1848.

Stow, John. *A Survey of London.* London, 1598; Everyman Library, 1929.

Thomas, A. H., and Thornley, I. D., eds. *The Great Chronicle of London.* London, 1887.

Education

Brown, J. Howard. *Elizabethan Schooldays*. Oxford, 1933.

Leach, A. F. *Educational Charters and Documents, 1598–1809*. Cambridge, 1911.

Mallet, C. E. *A History of the University of Oxford*. 3 vols. London, 1924–7.

Miller, Edward Haviland. *The Professional Writer in Elizabethan England*. Oxford, 1959.

Watson, Foster. *The English Grammar Schools to 1600: Their Curriculum and Practice*. Cambridge, 1908.

Wright, Louis B. *Middle-Class Culture in Elizabethan England*. Chapel Hill, N.C., 1935.

Lincoln's Inn

Ball, Sir William. *Lincoln's Inn: Its History and Tradition*. London, 1947.

Barton, D. Plunket, Benham, Charles, and Watt, Francis. *The Story of Our Inns of Court*. Boston and London, 1942.

Buck, Sir George. *The Third Universitie of England*. London, 1631.

A Catalogue of Pamphlets, Tracts, Proclamations, Speeches, Sermons, Trials, Petitions from 1500 to 1700, in the Library of the Honourable Society of Lincolns Inn. London, 1908.

Herbert, W. *Antiquities of the Inns of Court and Chancery*. London, 1804.

Home, Gordon, and Headlam, Cecil. *Inns of Court*. London, 1909.

Hurst, Sir Gerald. *Lincoln's Inn Essays*. London, 1949.

————. *A Short History of Lincoln's Inn*. London, 1941.

Spilsbury, William F. *Lincoln's Inn, Its Ancient and Modern*

Buildings, with an Accounting of Its Library. London, 1850.

Thorne, Samuel E., ed. *Readings and Moots at the Inns of Court in the Fifteenth Century*. London, 1954.

Walker, J. D., and Baildon, W. P. *The Black Books, The Records of the Honorable Society of Lincoln's Inn, 1422–1845*. 4 vols. London, 1897–1902.

Williams, E. *Early Holborn and the Legal Quarter of London*. 2 vols. London, 1927.

Justice of the Peace

Beard, Charles A. *The Office of Justice of the Peace in England, Its Origin and Development*. New York, 1904.

Crompton, Richard, rev. *LOffice et aucthoritie de Iustice de peace, in part collect per le iades treasureuvered Iudge, Monsieur A. Fitzherbert, et ore enlarge per Richard Crompton un Apprentice de le common ley & publie lan du grace, 1583*. London, 1583.

Cunningham, W., and Lamond, Elizabeth, eds. *A Discourse of the Common Weal of this Realm of England*. Cambridge, 1893.

Dalton, Michael. *The Country Justice*. London, 1618.

Furnivall, F. J. *William Stafford's Compendious or briefe Examination of certayne ordinary Complaints of our Countrymen in these our Dayes, A.D. 1581*. London, 1876.

Lambarde, William. *Eirenarcha*, London, 1581.

Osborne, Bertram. *Justices of the Peace 1361–1848*. Shaftsbury, 1960.

Putnam, Bertha Haven. *Early Treatises on the Practice of the Justices of the Peace in the Fifteenth and Sixteenth Centuries*. Oxford, 1926.

———. *Proceedings before the Justices of the Peace in the*

Fourteenth and Fifteenth Centuries from Edward III to Richard III. London, 1938.

Stephen, Sir James Fitzjames. *A History of the Criminal Law of England*. 3 vols. London, 1883.

Associates

Bowen, Catherine Drinker. *Francis Bacon, The Temper of a Man*. Boston, 1963.

———. *The Lion and the Throne: The Life and Times of Sir Edward Coke*. Boston, 1957.

Cecil, David Q. *Two Quiet Lives*. London, 1948.

Churton, Ralph. *The Life of Alexander Nowell, Dean of St. Paul's*. Oxford, 1809.

Douglas, David C. *English Scholars*. London, 1939.

Eland, D., ed. *Thomas Wotton's Letter-Book 1574–1586*. London, 1960.

Kittredge, George Lyman. *Witchcraft in Old and New England*. Cambridge, Massachusetts, 1929.

Montague, Basil, ed. *The Works of Francis Bacon*. London, 1836.

Smith, Logan Pearsall. *The Life and Letters of Sir Henry Wotton*. 2 vols. Oxford, 1907.

Twysdon, Sir John. *The Family of Twysdon or Twisdon*, Comp. C. H. Dudley. London, 1939.

Wilson, Sir Thomas. *The State of England*. London, 1600.

Law

Adams, G. B., and Stephens, H. M., eds. *Select Documents of English Constitutional History*. New York, 1947.

Allen, C. K. *Law in the Making*. 5th ed. Oxford, 1952.

Attenborough, F. L., ed. *The Laws of the Earliest English Kings*. Cambridge, 1922.

Bell, H. E. *An Introduction to the History and Records of the Court of Wards and Liveries.* Cambridge, 1953.

Bickley, Francis, ed. *Guide to the Reports of the Royal Commission.* London, 1852.

Black, Henry C. *Black's Law Dictionary.* St. Paul, Minn., 1951.

Blackstone, William. *Commentaries on the Laws of England.* 4 vols. London, 1765–9; Oxford, 1771.

Burns, John S., ed. *The Star Chamber.* London, 1870.

Cary, George. *Reports on Causes in Chancery, Collected . . . out of the Labours of Mr. William Lambert.* London, 1650, 1820.

Chrimes, S. B. *English Constitutional Ideas in the Fifteenth Century.* Cambridge, 1936.

Clarkson, Paul S., and Warren, Clyde T. *The Law of Property in Shakespeare and the Elizabethan Drama.* Baltimore, Md., 1942.

Coke, Sir Edward. *Second Institutes* (c. 1630). 4th ed. London, 1671.

Dasent, J. R., ed. *Acts of the Privy Council of England.* 32 vols. London, 1890–1907.

Davis, H. W., ed. *Stubb's Select Charters from the Beginning to 1307.* 9th ed. Oxford, 1870.

Dietz, F. C. *English Public Finance, 1558–1641.* New York, 1932.

Dugdale, William. *Origines Juridiciales, or Historical Memorials of the English Laws, Courts of Justice, &c.* London, 1666, 1671.

Greg, W. W. *Some Aspects and Problems of London Publishing Between 1550 and 1650.* Oxford, 1956.

Hardy, Thomas Duffes. *A Catalogue of Lord Chancellors.* London, 1843.

Hastings, Margaret. *The Court of Common Pleas in 15th Century England.* Ithaca, N.Y., 1947.

Herne, Jan. *The Law of Charitable Uses.* London, 1660.

Holdsworth, W. S. *A History of English Law.* 3 vols., London, 1903–9; 9 vols., 1922–6.

———. *Sources and Literature of English Law.* London, 1925.

Hurstfield, Joel. *The Queen's Wards.* London, 1958.

Jackson, R. M. *The Making of Justice in England.* Cambridge, 1940.

John, Eric. *Land Tenure in Early England.* Leicester, 1960.

Jordan, J. K. *Philanthropy in England.* London, 1959.

Keir, Sir David Lindsay. *The Constitutional History of Modern Britain 1485–1937.* London, 1948.

Lambarde, William. *Archeion,* eds. C. H. McIlwain and Paul L. Ward. Cambridge, Mass., 1957.

Leadam, I. S. *Select Cases in the Court of Requests.* London, 1898.

Lévy-Ullmann, Henri. *The English Legal Tradition.* London, 1935.

Liebermann, Felix. *On the Instituta Canuti aliorumque regnum Anglorum.* London, 1893.

Mackay, Thomas. *A History of the English Poor Laws.* London, 1904.

Maitland, F. W. *The Constitutional History of England.* Cambridge, 1908.

———. *The Court Baron.* London, 1891.

———. *English Law and the Renaissance.* Cambridge, 1901.

———. *Equity, Also the Forms of Action at Common Law.* Cambridge, 1909.

———. *The Forms and Action at Common Law.* Cambridge, 1936.

Monro, Cecil, ed. *Acta Cancellaria, or Selections from the Records of the Court of Chancery (1558–1624).* London, 1847.

Prothero, Sir G. W., ed. *Select Statutes and Other Documents.* London, 1894, 1949.

Richardson, H. C., and Sayles, G. O., eds. and trans. *Fleta.* London, 1955. Vol. II.

Saunders, G. W. *Orders of the High Court of Chancery.* London, 1727.

Somner, William. *A Treatise of Gavelkind.* London, 1660.

Spence, George. *The Equitable Jurisdiction of the Court of Chancery.* 2 vols. London, 1846.

Sweet, W. Harold, and Maxwell, Leslie F. *A Legal Bibliography of the British Commonwealth of Nations.* London, 1953.

Tanner, J. R. *Tudor Constitutional Documents, 1485–1603, with an Historical Commentary.* Cambridge, 1922, 1948.

Thorne, Samuel E., ed. *A Discourse upon the Exposicions & Understanding of Statutes with Sir Thomas Egerton's Additions.* San Marino, Cal., 1942.

Webb, Sidney and Beatrice. *The English Poor Laws.* London, 1927.

History

Bindoff, S. T. *Tudor England.* London, 1950.

Black, J. B. *The Reign of Queen Elizabeth, 1558–1603.* Oxford, 1959.

Brooks, F. W., ed. *Supplementary Stiffkey Papers,* Camden Miscellany, Third Series, LII (1936), 1–56, Introd.

Camden, William. *Annales rerum Anglicarum et Hibernicarum regnante Elizabetha . . . ad 1589.* London, 1615; Hearne, Thomas, ed. 3 vols., London, 1717.

———. *Britannia.* London, 1596.

Campbell, John Lord. *Lives of the Lord Chancellors and Keepers of the Great Seal of England . . . till the reign of George IV.* 7 vols., London, 1845–7; 10 vols., 1856–7.

Campbell, Mildred. *The English Yeoman under Elizabeth and the Early Stuarts.* New Haven, 1942.

Cheyney, Edward P. *A History of England: from the Defeat of the Armada to the Death of Elizabeth.* 2 vols. New York, 1914–26.

Collier, J. Payne, ed. *The Egerton Papers.* London, 1840.

Froude, J. A. *History of England from the Fall of Wolsey to the Defeat of the Spanish Armada.* 12 vols., London, 1856–70; revised ed., 12 vols., 1862–70.

Haller, William. *The Rise of Puritanism; or the Way to the New Jerusalem as Set Forth in the Pulpit and Press from Thomas Cartwright to John Lilburne and John Milton, 1570–1642.* New York, 1947.

Harman, Thomas. *A Caveat or Warening for Common Cursetors Vulgarly Called Vagabones.* London, 1567.

Harris, John. *The History of Kent, in Five Parts.* London, 1719.

Harrison, G. B., ed. *An Elizabethan Journal.* 2 vols. London, 1928–31.

Hull, Felix. *Guide to the Kent Archives Office.* Maidstone, 1958.

Hume, Martin. *The Courtships of Queen Elizabeth.* London, 1896, 1904.

———. *The Great Lord Burghley: A Study in Elizabethan Statecraft.* London, 1898, 1906.

Ireland, W. H. *England's Topographer.* 4 vols. London, 1828.

Karracker, Cyrus H. *The Seventeenth Century Sheriff.* Chapel Hill, N.C., 1930.

Knappen, Marshall M. *Tudor Puritanism.* Chicago, 1939.

Mackay, Thomas. *A History of the English Poor Laws.* London, 1904.

Mattingly, Garrett. *The Armada.* Boston, 1959.

Meyer, A. O. *England and the Catholic Church,* trans. J. R. McKee. London, 1916.

Mosse, George L. *The Struggle for Sovereignty in England.* Lansing, Mich., 1950.

Murray, K. M. E. *The Constitutional History of the Cinque Ports.* Manchester, 1935.

Neale, Sir John E. *Elizabeth I and Her Parliaments, 1584–1601.* 2 vols. London, 1953.

———. *The Elizabethan House of Commons.* London, 1949.

———. *Essays in Elizabethan History.* London, 1958.

———. *Queen Elizabeth.* London, 1934.

Nichols, John G., ed. *The Chronicle of Calais.* London, 1846.

Notestein, Wallace. *The English People on the Eve of Colonization.* New York, 1954.

Pickthorn, Kenneth. *Early Tudor Government.* Cambridge, 1934.

Pollard, A. E. *The Evolution of Parliament.* London, 1926.

———. *Factors in Modern History.* London, 1907.

———. *The Political History of England.* London, 1923.

Pollen, John H. *The English Catholics in the Reign of Queen Elizabeth.* London, 1920.

Read, Conyers. *Bibliography of British History, Tudor Period, 1485–1603.* Oxford, 1933, 1959.

———. *Mr. Secretary Cecil and Queen Elizabeth.* London, 1955.

———. *Mr. Secretary Walsingham and the Policy of Queen Elizabeth.* 3 vols. Oxford, 1925.

———. *The Tudors: Personalities and Politics in Sixteenth Century England.* New York, 1936.

———, ed. *William Lambarde and Local Government, His "Ephemeris" and Twenty-nine Charges to Juries and Commissions.* Folger Shakespeare Library Publications. Ithaca, N.Y., 1962.

Rowse, A. L. *The England of Queen Elizabeth.* New York, 1951.

Spedding, James, Ellis, R. L., and Heath, D. D. *The Letters and Life of Francis Bacon.* London, 1857–74, 1890.

Seton-Watson, R. W., ed. *Tudor Studies.* London, 1924.

Simpson, Percy. *Studies in Elizabethan Drama.* Oxford, 1955.

Smith, Alan Gordon. *The Babington Plot.* London, 1936.

Smith, Sir Thomas. *De Republica Anglorum, or a Discourse on the Commonwealth of England.* Cambridge, 1906.

Steinbicker, Carl R. *Poor-Relief in the Sixteenth Century.* Washington, D.C., 1937.

Strype, John. *Annals of the Reformation.* 4 vols. London, 1709–31; Oxford, 1820–40.

———. *The Life and Acts of John Whitgift, D.D.* 3 vols. Oxford, 1822.

———. *The Life and Acts of Matthew Parker.* 3 vols. London, 1711; Oxford, 1821.

Tawney, R. H. *The Agrarian Problem in the Sixteenth Century.* New York, 1912.

Tennison, E. M. *Elizabethan England: Being the History of This Country "In Relation to All Foreign Princes,"* from Original Manuscripts. . . . 10 vols. London, 1935–53.

Thomson, G. S., ed. *The Twysden Lieutenancy Papers 1583–1688.* Kent Archeological Society, 1926.

Twysden, Sir Roger. *Certaine Considerations upon the Government of England,* ed. J. M. Kemble. London, 1849.

Underhill, Arthur. *Shakespeare's England.* 2 vols. Oxford, 1916.

Willcox, William B. *Gloucestershire, A Study in Local Government 1590–1640.* New Haven, 1940.

INDEX

INDEX

INDEX

About the Author

Wilbur Dunkel, Professor of English at the University of Rochester since 1925, holds the master's degree from Harvard and the Ph.D. from the University of Chicago. He has done research at the Folger Shakespeare Library in Washington, and in 1960–61 was a Fellow at that institution. In addition to writing and teaching, he has conducted two lecture series on television, "Broadway Seminar" and "Shakespeare on Stage." His biography of Sir Arthur Pinero was published in 1941.

The type face used in the composition of both the text and display matter of this book is Caslon Old Face, with Caslon Openface on the title page. The book was printed by letterpress on 60# Mead Publishers' Imperial Text and bound in Columbia Title Vellum and Fictionette with endpapers of Multicolor Endleaf. It was manufactured by Quinn & Boden Company, Inc., Rahway, New Jersey.